Saturday Beans & Sunday Suppers

Kitchen Stories *from* Mary's Farm

Saturday Beans & Sunday Suppers

Kitchen Stories *from* Mary's Farm

BY EDIE CLARK

POWERSBRIDGE PRESS

PETERBOROUGH, NEW HAMPSHIRE

Some parts of this book have appeared in different form in *Yankee* magazine, for which I'm grateful.

Book design: Jill Shaffer
Title page illustration of Edie's Glenwood stove: Erick Ingraham

First printing October 2007
10 9 8 7 6 5 4 3 2 1 paperback

Publisher's Cataloging-in-Publication Data
  Clark, Edie, 1948–
    Saturday Beans & Sunday Suppers / Edie Clark
      p.   cm.
  ISBN 0-9719934-5-9
    1. Essays — gastronomy — New England.   I. Title.
    641—dc22

Powersbridge Press
P.O. Box 332
Peterborough, NH 03458

Ordering information: www.edieclark.com

I*t seems to me that our three basic needs, for food and security and love, are so mixed and mingled and entwined that we cannot straightly think of one without the others. So it happens that when I write of hunger, I am really writing about love and the hunger for it, and warmth and the love of it and the hunger for it . . . and then the richness and fine reality of hunger satisfied . . . and it is all one.*

M.F.K. FISHER

Contents

Acknowledgments

I am most grateful to Mel Allen, Martha White, Jill Shaffer, Steve Lewers, Katrina Kenison, Sue Callihan, Erick Ingraham, Liz Meryman, Vicki Stiefel, Lida Stinchfield, Kin Schilling, Mac Odell, Susan Odell Hand, George Odell, all helpers in the kitchen of my words.

Introduction

WHEN I SAT DOWN to write this book, I believed I was going to write about some favorite New England foods and include the recipes for each. But as the book progressed, I realized that food cannot be separated from place and memory, family and events from the past. In a way, then, there is no more powerful memoir than the food itself, a sensory cue strong enough to conjure the past as present, the present as past. Aromas and touch can bring back the pageant of what came before.

We all must have that big bundle of saved recipes, stashed in an accordion file or a bulging recipe box — how many times have I said I would organize them so I could more easily find what I am looking for? And yet I don't do it. Perhaps this constant disarray of clippings and handwritten instructions is essential to the confusion of the many dishes we serve up as life. I have Rhubarb Cake, written out in my (first) mother-in-law's handwriting. She does not identify the recipe as hers, but I know her telltale script as well as my own. When I open the file (the binding blown out from the pressure of all those saved receipts), recipes for Seville Orange Marmalade, carefully typed and signed from Martha Chace, fall out along with a recipe for Spoon Bread from a restaurant in Harlem and one for Oatmeal Orange Muffins (the card says it is my own recipe, though I don't remember when or why I made it up); Gretel Ehrlich's Sweet Potato Biscuits; Martha Stewart's Cloud Pancakes (which I copied down while watching her TV show early one Sunday morning — it remains one of my favorites). Between seemingly endless cutouts from the *Boston Globe* and the *New York Times* are tucked neighbor Peg Colony's recipe for Jalapeño Cornbread, Cranberry Relish from NPR, and *Soupe au Pistou* from dear friend Geneviève, a native of Provence. Kefir, Strawberry Pie, Pork Loin, Beef Bourguignon, crabcakes, *tiramisu*, jerk chicken and Key Lime Pie. It all adds up to an incredible feast, not only for the palate but also for the mind, a brew of memory and friends unlike anything any other part of my life could provide. Food, made by our own hands or passed to us from loved ones, is, without parallel and without guise, our lifeblood. It is what creates us, mind and body and spirit. Some food is simply nourishment, passed to us through a window of a fast-food chain and eaten from our laps as we navigate traffic. This is hardly food, only fuel, and even that is questionable nourishment. Food created by us and for us is our substance, the essence of love and reminiscence.

And so, while writing this book, I have lived another lifetime and then some, serving forth not so much the food but the memories of other places, other times, other people. While writing, I found myself in the dining room of a hotel in northern Scotland with my aunt and uncle, now passed away; on a hike through wilderness woods, which ended with a swim in a remote reservoir, water clear as air; working on the crew of a church bean supper, eating the leftovers after all have been served, the kitchen gone quiet; eating roast lamb at a long wooden table, shoulder to shoulder with the other family members and neighbors with whom I'd just clipped a herd of Icelandic sheep. Can I ever eat roast lamb without thinking of that midnight meal?

And so it was that my simple book of favorite foods and recipes transformed into a palimpsest, the diverse layers of life and love, decade on decade, hidden beneath the surface of a good meal, well served, and the recipes, here shared.

Edie Clark
Harrisville, New Hampshire
June 2007

PART ONE

The Sixties

Aunt Peg's Chowder

THE WEEKEND AFTER I graduated from college, I went to visit my aunt Peg in Shirley Center, Massachusetts. The year was 1970 and for the past ten years, my aunt and uncle and my beloved cousins had lived in a big center-chimney Colonial house that had an interesting-enough history to have been included in a book about architecture. Growing up, I loved spending all the time I could there. My cousin George and I loved exploring the "secret" room where they said fugitive slaves had hidden as they passed along the Underground Railroad. The rooms went 'round in a circle, upstairs and down, so that you had to walk through other bedrooms in order to get to the bathroom. Every room, as I recall, had a fireplace in it and in the living room there was a fireplace big enough to walk into. A crane for hanging cast-iron kettles was poised over the hearth, and on either side of the fireplace wooden panels fit tightly into domed openings: brick

ovens. The floors creaked and the multipaned, wavy glass windows
leaked cold air throughout the long winters. The kitchen, which
was the center of my aunt's home, was not really in the center, but
in the ell, off the dining room. That room was always warm and
it was there that we spent so much time together. It was my aunt,
never my mother, who had taught me what I knew to date about
cooking, and on that day in June of 1970, I was anticipating setting up my first kitchen in an apartment I had agreed to rent in
downtown Philadelphia. "Come on," Aunt Peg said. "Let's find
some recipes to get you started."

Aunt Peg kept all her recipes, handwritten on index cards,
in a small box that she stashed in one of the many wooden cupboards of that wondrous kitchen of my early memories. She
went to the cupboard and pulled out the box, which I recall with
pleasure, made of honey-colored wood, the sides stained, not in
an unsightly way but as if the box had made a pleasant journey
through its apparently long life. The familiar box had accompanied my adventurous aunt through her years, which began in an
apartment in Greenwich Village, where she lived with my uncle
Jamie until the war years. Then they moved to Washington,
D.C., so my uncle could be near the Pentagon, where he worked
throughout World War II.

After the war ended, they began their life in Massachusetts,
which seems to be where they felt they belonged, though they had
no roots there — my aunt grew up in New Jersey, as did most of
my family, and my uncle grew up in Illinois. My aunt was not a
New Englander by birth, but it was from her, and from my uncle,

that I developed my love for New England. I sometimes think that what we love about New England is its evocation of the past. It is a region that reminds us of another time, another place, and we cling to that, hopefully. Whatever it was that brought them here, they both developed a passionate allegiance to New England. In the early 1950s, they found a spot to live on the North Shore of Boston where they embraced the sea and the rocky shores of that happy time in our nation's history. Eventually my uncle's work brought him to central Massachusetts, where they settled into that pre-Revolutionary home. Doors separated all the rooms and moving from one room to another involved a sharp *clack*, an announcement of your arrival. Big logs sometimes smoked silently through the afternoon in more than one fireplace. The fire was a presence in the house and outside the back door was a long row of stacked logs, each log so big only one could be carried in at a time. And usually that one was tossed, with a *thunk* and a cloud of sparks, on top of the fading embers of the last. My aunt and uncle's love of New England, its history, its lifestyle, its foods, was palpable. Their house spoke it with all its curious sections, keeping rooms and back ells, the "out back" and the "way out back," which was their way of identifying the first attached shed and the second. The rabbit shed sat on a rise behind the house. I have no idea what its original purpose was — maybe indeed it was a home for rabbits — but in my time it was where an overflow of overnight guests could stay, summer only.

I can imagine that, just as the patina on the little recipe box grew richer, the volume of the index cards increased as my aunt encountered one meal after another. She loved to entertain and loved to be entertained. A tall and slender woman whose weight remained stable throughout her eighty-nine years, Aunt Peg made no bones about the fact that she loved to eat. Although she was a thinking woman who embraced radical thinking almost in reaction to her civilized upbringing, food seemed to be the kernel of her life. At any time of crisis, large or small, Aunt Peg brought out the food — good, warm, comforting dishes that she knew could not solve the problem but which she knew could soothe it.

That day, she brought the box out to the dining room table and we sat down together. I had a pen and a stack of brand-new index cards onto which I could copy the recipes of my choice. We sorted through her cards, looking specifically for concoctions that were easy, cheap, and delicious. She understood that my mother, her sister, had not given me many advantages in the kitchen and my aunt was sympathetic to my limitations. I had my favorites for starters. Cheese Strata was a dish my aunt often made. "There isn't anything easier than that," she proclaimed and passed the card my way. Another favorite was Fish Chowder. Orange Marmalade Soufflé. Iced Tea. She dealt them out like a hand of cards. My collection had begun.

Of all the recipes transferred to my care that day, Fish Chowder was the one I loved and used the most. Once I took up residence in that small studio apartment in Philadelphia, I began to invite friends over for dinner. This also was new territory for me. My mother's dislike for cooking had the residual effect of preventing her from doing any kind of entertaining. Whatever was to be done in the kitchen she hoped could be done swiftly and without making a mess. She kept dinners simple and confined to a narrow menu. Baked chicken and baked potatoes appeared often on our dinner table and Jell-O was a frequent dessert. My mother's attitude toward food seemed to be the root of the quiet life we led. Parties or gatherings rarely took place at our house.

Not so my aunt's, which is likely one reason why I loved going there. From Aunt Peg, I learned of the warmth that comes back to you when you provide a good meal for friends. Fish chowder was the first dish I was able to make with pride, in my new kitchen, my new life. In fact, I served that chowder so often I came to call it Aunt Peg's Chowder. I've given the recipe out to many friends and told them of the day that Aunt Peg and I sat down at that table in her big old creaky-floor house and I copied the recipe onto cards of my own.

One winter Sunday, a couple of years before my aunt died, she and my uncle came north from their home in Massachusetts to have lunch with me. This was always a very special occasion to me, the chance to host them in my own home, the chance to give back just a little of all that they had given me over the years. They did not come often, but whenever they did, I took special care in cleaning the house and planning out the menu. What to serve was a big puzzle. More than thirty years had passed since I had received that little stash of "easy" recipes on that June day in 1970, and in the meantime I had added substantially to my personal recipe book. Because it was a relatively long drive, they usually came just for lunch. As discerning as they both were in the kitchen, they were always more than gracious in their enthusiasm for what I served, especially the homemade bread, which they both ate with gusto.

That day, I decided to serve Aunt Peg's chowder. As I steamed the fish and cut up the potatoes, I thought nostalgically of that day when she bestowed the recipe on me and realized, somewhat in amazement, that in spite of the many, many satisfied guests who had enjoyed this chowder, I couldn't recall ever having served it to Aunt Peg. I couldn't wait to surprise her with her own recipe. In addition to the chowder, I made Anadama Bread, which was both my uncle's favorite and my father's. I sliced the bread on a board and set it on the table. Then I placed the steaming bowls in front of her and Uncle Jamie, waiting for them to recognize it. "Fish chowder," they said, at once, "What a treat!" They dipped their spoons in.

"This is interesting," Uncle Jamie said. "I don't think I've ever had fish chowder with corn *and* potatoes in it."

"Neither have I," remarked Aunt Peg. "But it's really very good. Where did you get the recipe?"

"But," I said, "this is the recipe *you* gave me. Don't you remember?"

"No, dearie," she said, in the gentle but firm way she had of contradicting. "I've never made a chowder like this."

I searched back into my memory. Could there be any doubt that I had gotten this recipe from her? I thought not. I even had the same old recipe card, stained now from years of kitchen spills.

I protested: "I even call it Aunt Peg's Chowder!"

"Well, but it's *not!*"

I got nowhere. They loved the chowder and even wanted the recipe, please. I still believe this is Aunt Peg's recipe but she would not claim it. And if it did not come from her, I can't imagine who gave it to me. Whoever it was, it's a great recipe for a wonderful milk chowder, tried and loved for as many years as I've been cooking on my own. ·

Not Aunt Peg's Fish Chowder

1 pound fish such as cod or haddock

1 cup cold water

2 cups potatoes, cubed, cooked

1 onion, chopped

½ cup water

1 cup corn kernels, fresh, frozen or canned

3 cups milk

1 teaspoon salt

fresh ground pepper

1 tablespoon butter

salt pork

Place the fish and the water into a good-sized soup pot or kettle and simmer for ten minutes. Add the potatoes, the onion, ½ cup water and the corn. Simmer for another ten minutes, then add the milk, salt and fresh ground pepper to taste. Bring this just to the boiling point, but do not allow to boil. Turn off the heat, add the butter and taste for salt. Serve hot with bits of fried salt pork on top and Pilot crackers. Serves 6.

The Magic Brew

WHEN IT WAS HOT OUT, my aunt and I used to go out and sit under the shade of the towering maple that edged the open foundation of a big old barn, a structure that certainly had not stood within my memory. Instead, there was a broad rectangle of man-sized boulders, all perfectly balanced, one on the other, that kept the memory of the barn I'd never seen. A circle of comfortable lawn chairs beside this sunken wall was where we retreated in times of extreme heat. Usually we'd sit there a while and talk about this and that before Aunt Peg would finally say, "Shall we make up a pitcher of iced tea?" I was always waiting for her to ask and anxious to take part.

We'd rise from our chairs and go inside and start to make the tea, which she claimed once saved a young boy's life. For this lifesaver, bags of lemons and oranges seemed always at the ready in the refrigerator. I'd go for them without being told. We worked side by side, cutting up lemons and oranges and then squeezing them in the Juicerette, a strong-arm hand juicer from the 1930s, whose design, my aunt and I decided, had yet to be improved upon. "If they can't think of a better way, why change it?" Aunt Peg would say, as she slid an orange half into the jaw of the juicer and clamped down on the handle with a mighty push. Droplets popped into the air and the release of juice gushed into the stainless-steel bowl she had placed underneath to catch the bounty. The mechanism also cleverly strained out the seeds, removing that part of our job. Pretty soon, that big old kitchen smelled like a citrus grove.

Rinds piled up on the counter as we worked, lemons topping the oranges. When we had enough juice, we cut the rinds in small pieces and transferred them into her well-used, twin-handled kettle, the pot that also made wonderful soups and chilis and steamed vegetables, everything good. My aunt used it so often, it never was put away but instead sat on one of the stove burners, ready for action at all times. My aunt took the kettle in both hands and held it under the faucet, covering the rinds with well water. It was wonderful water, maybe my favorite thing in that entire kitchen. At home, we had municipal water that went through a treatment system before arriving in our sink. It smelled and I disliked the taste and always looked forward to being at Aunt Peg's, where the water seemed pure and actually tasted good.

My aunt turned on the burner. I loved watching the colorful rinds floating on the surface of the clear water, a tropical display. While we waited for the water to boil, my aunt would sometimes sit down at the piano, which was just outside the kitchen, and play a little bit or, when I got a little older, she would ask me to do that. And we'd play or sit on the bench and read some of the music that sat in a tall pile beside the piano.

Eventually the water would boil, and in the same way, the fragrance of lemons and oranges mixed together would fill up the sultry summer air all around us. The water would slowly move the rinds here and there as they simmered.

"Measure out the sugar, dearie," Aunt Peg would say and I'd hurry to the cupboard and get down the big tin that held enough sugar for a safari. Using the tin cup measure, I poured the crystals in as slowly as my small hands could manage, while Aunt Peg stirred the brew with a wooden spoon. "Good!" she said and then I went for the tea. I pretty much knew the drill. With a tablespoon measure, I added the hard, curled leaves, sprinkling them like seasoning across the swirling sea of citrus.

And with that, Aunt Peg would turn off the burner and carry the pot over to the wooden board, where it would sit and steep and cool. And we'd go back to our chairs beneath the big maple to sit and steep and cool.

I had learned that the next part of the recipe was patience. The tea had to cool a little bit. Otherwise, no ice would last a second in the glass. But it was a fidgety time. Sometimes, we got so impatient we would decide it was a good time to go to the store and pick up a few items for dinner. Or maybe walk to the post office. I was always barefoot in those days and recall the pleasant feel of the soft road tar under my feet as we walked on a hot day. My tall aunt strode beside me in her comfortable tie shoes. The walk was always rewarded with a chat with the postmistress, Mrs. Bull, who enjoyed catching up with my aunt, and then there was sometimes a letter from my mother or my grandmother, a bonus.

When we got home, I'd check the sides of the pot to find it was cool. I'd hold the colander steady while my aunt strained the concoction into the big pitcher. And into the fridge it would go. Another dollop of patience was needed at this point. The tea was never made quickly and so it always made sense to make more than we thought we would drink. And try to remember to make it before the hottest part of the day. But the trouble was, our brew never made it to the end of the day.

The tea was our constant companion. It went with us on picnics. It was with us on boats, on hikes and in the car. It was served at breakfast, lunch and dinner and in between, all summer long and into the fall. We always hoped that there would be some left over but there rarely was. If we wanted more, we had to start all over again with the juicer and the loose tea.

In fact, this concoction was not of my aunt's devising. I don't suppose any recipe really comes from any one person and I have no way of knowing what, if anything, she contributed to the method. It came to her from my uncle's side of the family, a recipe that came with the marriage, if you will, like a mother-in-law or a set of silver. So it had further lineage. But for me, the recipe belonged to Aunt Peg and was a part of her legend, which seemed to grow the longer I stood at her side, my young mind forming its opinions, likes and dislikes. More than just a drink, it was an elixir, a potion, a magic brew.

My aunt's story of how her iced tea saved a life goes something like this: A young man in the neighborhood used to come every week to mow their lawn. When he stopped for a break, Aunt Peg would bring him a glass of her iced tea, which, like all the rest of us, he had learned to crave. One summer, the boy became ill and was taken to the hospital, where he fell into a coma. When at last he began to show signs of life, he was asked if he wanted anything. Barely conscious, he croaked out in hard-to-decipher tones: "Mrs. Odell's iced tea." My aunt was called and she quickly concocted a big batch of her famous tea, which she carried in to his hospital room in a glass jug.

One sip at a time, one day at a time, the young boy revived and eventually recovered completely. Of course, whether or not the tea saved his life would be impossible to prove, but that is how the story went and we all believed it like gospel. Who wouldn't? We knew that tea. We had all been witnesses to its reviving powers. It was a magic brew that could make a cadaver rise up and dance.

And so it is, when the sun sends us onto the screened porch for relief, I get out the kettle and start brewing. The smell of tea and oranges and lemons will always take me back to those summers in my aunt's kitchen in the 1960s. The recipe probably had other amazing chapters but, like the old barn foundation out under the big maple, I knew of it only in my own way. Over the years, I've shared this recipe with so many friends and I usually tell the story of the young boy when I serve it. If my friends have never had the tea before, they nod and smirk. But after that first glass, they pretty much know that what I say is true.

Aunt Peg's Iced Tea

2 lemons

1 orange

1 cup sugar

2 tablespoons loose black tea

Squeeze the lemons and the orange and set the juice aside. Cut the peels into small pieces and cover with two cups of water. Cook for five minutes, until the juice is out of the peels. Add the sugar and the tea. Remove from the heat and steep for several minutes. Strain. Add the orange and lemon juices and four cups of water. Chill. Serves 8. It's so good, you will want to double or triple the recipe.

A Vermont Mystery

ATRIP TO VISIT MY AUNT in the winter always
involved skiing. In fact, there were times when that
was the sole reason for my visit. Their home in central Massachusetts made them relatively close to many of the developing Vermont ski areas back in the late 1950s and early 1960s. That in itself
was a small miracle to me, since traveling to those places from my
home in New Jersey would have meant a very long journey. Being
at my aunt's, the mountains seemed like next-door neighbors and
so, whenever I had a school vacation, I went north to be with my
cousins. I had learned to ski with them when I was ten or twelve,
at Priest's, a small backyard ski hill complete with a rope tow. That
was fine for an afternoon, but once the big mountains started
offering challenging trails, my aunt and uncle felt the longer drive
was well worth it. I collected patches from those early destina-
tions, which I later sewed onto my ski parka. Bromley. Mount
Snow. Stowe. Cannon. Okemo. These were all in their infancy at

that time. The mountains have stood unchanged but the lodges were sometimes just big open spaces, usually with a fireplace that held enormous logs and a small concession stand that sold simple sandwiches, chips and soda. Sometimes hot chocolate. Being of the thrifty sort, my aunt always packed our lunch, which was better than anything we could buy anyway.

The day started early. In the dark of the early morning, Cousin George and I would pile into the backseat. Uncle Jamie secured our skis to the roof and off we'd go, a merry cargo northward bound. George and I kept our boots next to us on the seat, to make sure they would be warm when it came time to put them on. Depending on which mountain we chose, the trip was sometimes a couple of hours. As we drove, the light dawned and we watched as the snow banks grew higher and higher the further north we drove. In Vermont at that time, the roads were snow-covered, all the time, so I can well remember the silence of our journey, as the tires whispered along the snow pack. Aunt Peg would often read to us out loud, from a long book, perhaps Mark Twain, or, if it was on a Sunday, she read to us from the Bible. That always intrigued me because I didn't think of her or anyone in the family as being particularly religious — just regular churchgoers. Perhaps she felt that it was a good way to make up for the fact that skiing on Sunday eliminated the opportunity to go to church. No one but a minister had ever read scripture to me out loud.

So we'd travel along on the winding, snow-carpeted roads, Uncle Jamie behind the wheel and Aunt Peg sitting half turned toward him and half facing us in the backseat, so we could all hear the story. She often paused to comment or ask questions, especially when she was reading from the Bible, which often didn't make sense to me, at least not the first time through.

My uncle always knew exactly how much time we had before arriving at the mountain, and he would give me and George a ten-minute warning to get our boots on. Once we got there, we wanted to get out of the car and be on the slopes as fast as we could, to take advantage of all the skiing possible. We always tried to get there just as the ticket office was opening and ski to the very last run of the day. So, on with the boots and out of the car, George and I racing each other to the gate. Even when he was very young, George was a graceful, fearless skier and he always left me behind after the first run. These new mountains had J bars and T bars at that time; I don't recall any of them having chairlifts until a few years later. Before we knew it, we were up the mountain in the cold air and then flying down the hill.

Skiing made us hungry. The lunch my aunt Peg packed was always good but simple. Sandwiches ranged from peanut butter and jelly to sharp cheddar, lettuce and mayonnaise sandwiches. The bread was always good. Sometimes, if there had been a ham for dinner, there was a slice of ham in there. Always apples or oranges and a tall Thermos of hot chocolate. We'd clomp into the lodge in our rigid boots, find a space on a bench and wolf it down as fast as we could so we could get back out onto the trails. The day always whizzed by in fairy-tale time. Now and again, we would meet up on a trail and Aunt Peg would reach into her parka pouch and bring out a chocolate bar. For each of us, she broke off a little chunk, "for energy," she'd say. We'd quickly down the treat before continuing our runs. After the lifts closed, we piled back into the car and headed home, usually to enjoy a late supper at the house.

And now is the mystery. One year we were heading home from one of the mountains and we stopped at a little gas station, one old pump and a small red-and-white station. It had a big, round metal sign swinging from a post by the side of the road and in all ways looked just like any other gas station. That much is clear as day. My uncle got out and went inside while the station attendant filled our tank with gas. Uncle Jamie returned and said, "Let's all go inside and get something to eat." This was unusual as we didn't often stop for dinner on the way home. That was considered extravagant. Inside the station was the usual counter with the phone and the cash register. Behind it, as I recall, was a red-checked curtain. Uncle Jamie motioned us to come through the curtain with him. Behind the curtain was a small room with two or three round tables, like a little café, with big windows looking out on a snow-covered landscape, spruce trees and hills. Around the windows, small white lights twinkled at us. A potbellied stove at the back of the room was pumping out warmth. The tables were covered with red-checked cloths. We settled at the table in the corner, near the big window, placing our ski jackets over the backs of our chairs. A woman wearing a full apron and a big smile entered through the curtains.

"Bon soir!" she said and my uncle took right up with her in what French he had. I was taking French lessons in school so I listened intently but was disheartened to find I could not understand anything they said. There were no menus but he ordered for us all. After she left, he looked at us with his best mischievous

expression and said, "I wanted to surprise you all! I have heard they have wonderful French Onion Soup."

Hearing this, I was not so excited. What was that, I wondered. It sounded dull.

"What is French Onion Soup, Uncle Jamie?" I asked.

"You'll find out, Edie!" my fun-loving uncle answered and gave me his wink. In years to come, Uncle Jamie was to become my gustatory companion but that was yet to be revealed.

After some time, the French-speaking woman returned through the curtain, four steaming bowls crowding her tray. The arresting aroma of toasted cheese and onions shot through the wood-heated air. Using a hot mitt, she placed a bowl in front of me. The bowl was more like a small casserole, brown pottery with a small handle on the side. A cascade of browned, melted cheese was rippled, almost volcanic as it oozed down the side of the dish. We all took up our spoons like miners going after a new vein. Our eagerness was repelled at once by the intense heat of the cheese, which almost audibly sizzled on our tongues. We dug our spoons back in our bowls and lifted them again. Strings of cheese attached to our spoons and clung to the bowls. Uncle Jamie stretched his spoon upward to arm's length, exaggerating the effect of the lively, hot cheese. We sat, impatiently waiting for the soup to cool, at last taking small spoonfuls, blowing on them before tasting.

Even all these years later, I can remember the sensation of pleasure that soup evoked. It was thick, rich, cheesy and creamy, with the sweetness of the onions blended in. The bread and the broth had turned into a light, puffy entity all its own. Like nothing

I had ever tasted. Now I think, maybe it was the surprise, the atmosphere of the tiny, hidden dining room behind the gas station. While we blew on our soup, other skiers had joined us in the wood-heated sanctuary. Everyone was eating the French woman's soup. She was, my uncle told us, the wife of the mechanic. French, not French Canadian, but from France, and she had come here and married this man. To enhance his business, she started selling her soup to ski travelers who stopped to buy gas or have their engines repaired. And without much in the way of advertising (I recall no signs that revealed that an incredible culinary treat waited behind that country curtain), she was able to bring in the skiers. Day after day, week after week.

The trouble with that story is that I don't remember anything else about that day, such as what mountain we were skiing. It might have been Suicide Six, up near Woodstock, Vermont. Maybe Bromley. But I don't know. We never returned to the gas station/café but I never forgot the flavor of that soup. Some years later, when I was all grown up and working for *Yankee* magazine, I remembered the café and asked my uncle about it. I wondered if it might still exist. To my surprise, since he was always the source of all kinds of trivial information and remembered almost everything, he couldn't recall where that was. He did remember the day, and the soup, but he couldn't remember exactly where it was. My aunt could not remember either, nor could my cousin. When on assignment for *Yankee,* on drives up through Vermont, especially when I was on Route 100, I would slow and scan the roadsides, looking for the old gas pump and the red-and-white garage. It seemed unlikely the old couple would still be in there, but it became a kind of fantasy, a Vermont hope that I would find it and go inside, where, behind the curtain, world-class French Onion Soup would be served to me by a cheerful, aproned French woman in a wood-heated room decorated with twinkle lights. But I never found it. Perhaps it was a fleeting marriage and the woman returned to France. At least we all remembered the soup. And that day.

Since I couldn't find the garage, I decided to try to recover the soup itself. (My aunt did make French onion soup but it was always a disappointment, definitely not her strength.) I scanned a number of cookbooks, looking under French Onion Soup and made a few of those recipes but most were thin and watery. Most commonly, these recipes were nothing more than clear, onion-flavored broth sprinkled with croutons and Parmesan cheese. None even came close to my memory of that long ago treat. Finally, I found a recipe in a vegetarian cookbook published in the 1970s for hippies. It called for baguette and sour cream, cheese and lots of onions. And perhaps the secret ingredients: lemon juice and cognac. I made the soup and it was so close, I made it again and again for friends and neighbors, fine-tuning it until it had that thick richness of a casserole. At last, I made it for my French-speaking friend, Geneviève, who came to this country from France in the 1960s, when she was nineteen. "Where did you get this recipe?" she breathed in low tones, making the most of her dramatically inflected French accent. "This is the real thing!" she exclaimed.

Sometimes it takes so long to find what we are looking for. After all those years of searching, I had found the soup and turned it into a surprise of my own. By then, my aunt and uncle had passed away and who knows whatever did happen to that Vermont roadside café. But the memory was rich and, unlike many memories, it grew into a reality that is alive and well in my kitchen now. So often, my French Onion Soup is served with salad. And beer, which is how my uncle liked it.

French Onion Soup

4 large or 6 medium onions

3 tablespoons olive oil

4 cups chicken, beef or vegetable broth

2 cups water

1 bay leaf

½ teaspoon thyme or herbes de Provence

2 teaspoons lemon juice

2 tablespoons brandy

salt and fresh ground pepper

sliced baguette, stale or fresh

1 cup sour cream

½ cup each grated Gruyère and Parmesan cheese

Cut the onions in half, slice and cut in half again. Sauté in the olive oil slowly until the onions are very tender. Add broth, water, herbs, lemon juice and brandy. Add salt and pepper to taste and simmer slowly for ½ to 1 hour. In a large casserole, arrange slices of the French bread. Top each slice with a generous tablespoon of sour cream. Add the cheeses. When the soup is ready, pour it over the bread. Bake the soup in a hot oven (375 degrees) for 15 to 20 minutes, until the cheese is browned. Serves 6.

Au Bon Table Fitchburg

W HEN MY MOTHER DIED, my sister and I cleaned out the cupboards of her kitchen and found that all the spices and herbs in the spice cabinet she had been given when she and my father married, nearly fifty years beforehand, remained unopened. Similarly, I have my mother's edition of *The Joy of Cooking*, given to her for her wedding. The spine is barely cracked, the pages crisp and unturned. In short, my mother was not interested in food or anything that surrounded it.

By contrast, visiting my aunt's house was something like traveling to a foreign country where everything, most especially in the kitchen, was completely different and thus an adventure. Her cupboards were active places where interesting ingredients were not only stashed but frequently used: dry mustard, saffron, cinnamon sticks, real cocoa powder. The shelves were lightly dusted with grains of all the busy spices, coming and going. The list is very long and probably not as surprising now, as we are all educated gourmands, but back in those days, these discoveries were unusual and exciting. Most everything my aunt made I considered to be exciting. Roast beef was not just roast beef, but it was accompanied by Yorkshire Pudding. Hollandaise sauce was served often, mostly over asparagus but sometimes in the morning as Eggs Benedict. Welsh rarebit with beer was a favorite Sunday supper that followed our ski excursions. Steak and kidney pie was sometimes served for dinner guests. Apple pie was a staple. Vichysoisse. A favorite salad was fresh green beans, cooked but not to the point of exhaustion, cooled and tossed in the salad bowl with fresh sliced tomatoes from the garden. Every salad was dressed with Aunt Peg's signature vinaigrette, which she taught me to make while I was in college. One very cold January day I had stopped by on my way north to a cabin in Maine where I was going to spend a few days with friends. Afraid we would starve out there in the wilderness, she packed up a basket of essentials, among them a jar of vinaigrette. "Two parts oil, one part red wine vinegar, salt and pepper and a clove of garlic, crushed and left in the dressing," she recited as she measured it all out into a jar that once held peanut butter. "And fresh parsley if you have it. It's easy to remember and easy to make. You can take this with you wherever you go and always have good dressings for your salads."

Indeed, I have taken that wherever I have gone, ever since, and her words have never failed me and the vinaigrette never failed either of us. Her French-inspired recipe was one of the stones of her kitchen foundation. Throughout her long life, I never knew her to serve any other kind of dressing.

My aunt's fervor in the kitchen did bring forth New England dishes at times but, I am surprised to remember, more often brought forth concoctions with French roots. Since no one in our family was from France, I'm pretty sure this could also be called a New England trend as my aunt, along with a legion of other housewives of that era, had taken up the flag of Julia Child and begun to salute. I recall watching Julia Child's early television shows with Aunt Peg. I sat on an old wooden stool that I favored and my aunt sat in the small armchair in her study, facing the television, which was black and white and had a handle on top, so it could be lifted and carried to other rooms. Big rabbit ears shot up from the top of the box and the screen was not much bigger than a dinner plate. She rarely watched television so her attention to this show was notable. As Julia ranged about the kitchen, in her passionate yet careless manner, whacking chickens up onto the counter, grabbing hot dishes without a glove (resulting in a shriek), dropping the butter onto the floor, my aunt absorbed all of this as if studying for a course on which she would be tested. In the same way, I would often find her sitting in the living room, absorbed in the text of *The Art of French Cooking*. The result was a lot of French dishes, some of which were very good, some of which needed perhaps a few more trials. Not all of her French-style dishes remained on her agenda. I recently asked my cousin Susan about my aunt's fascination with French cooking, which I had not thought much about until I began writing this book. The hollandaise. The vinaigrette. The béarnaise sauce. Aside from all this home study, my aunt had apparently taken a course in French cooking in nearby Fitchburg, of all places, a course to which Julia Child had apparently given her blessings from afar. I never knew of this but it all added up to a very exotic repertoire inside Aunt Peg's house.

One of the desserts Aunt Peg enjoyed surprising her guests with was Orange Marmalade Soufflé. I think she wanted me to learn that something that sounds so elegant can really be quite easy. Well, I don't know if that is why she wanted me to know how to make it but it is how I think of it now. Certainly, for me, different — at home, our desserts were most often Jell-O or applesauce from the jar.

And so, when it came time for dessert, Aunt Peg would rise from the table and say, "Let's make Orange Marmalade Soufflé!" I already knew this was coming because, as with all meals, she would always map out our course with me early in the day, the main dish, the vegetables, the dessert. But on her command, we would all go into the kitchen and one of us would get out the double boiler, another would start separating the eggs (carefully saving the egg yolks for the next night's hollandaise sauce) and another would get out the sugar and the marmalade. I recall that if my cousin Susan, who was much older, was home from college, she would take charge as this particular dish was a favorite of hers. Within minutes, we would have impressed ourselves with an elegant confection, ready to eat. Whipped cream — what my aunt always called the *pièce de résistance* — was spooned on top of the pretty, puffy dome after we'd slid it, warm, onto a platter. We went back to our seats around the table and held out our plates, each of us hungry for our share.

Orange Marmalade Soufflé

4 egg whites

4 tablespoons sugar

4 tablespoons orange marmalade

whipping cream

Gradually add the sugar as you beat the egg whites till they peak (add a pinch of salt while you beat). Fold in the marmalade. Place water in the bottom of a good-sized double boiler and put over heat on the stove. Grease the top of the double boiler and place in the bottom. When the water in the bottom is boiling, pour the soufflé mixture into the top. Reduce the heat and cook the soufflé gently for 30 to 45 minutes. It will rise and it should be firm when it's done. While it's cooking, whip the cream. Invert onto a pretty dish and serve hot, with whipped cream on top. Serves 4.

Vinegar Cake

ONE MORNING when I was about ten years old, my
mother told me that Aunt Genee was coming to visit
us. She lived in Pennsylvania and did not come often. In addition,
it was her birthday.

"Let's make Aunt Genee a cake!" I exclaimed.

My mother was less than enthusiastic about that idea but I
begged until she relented. If cakes were ever made in our house,
they were from a mix. I wanted to find a recipe for a layer cake
and make it from scratch, as it seemed like a very special occasion.
For Christmas, the year before, my grandmother had given me
a Betty Crocker cookbook for children. It was spiral bound and
had a smooth vinyl cover. In it were recipes for Pigs in Blankets,
Peanut Butter Cremes and Sloppy Joes. And chocolate layer cake.
I set to work and followed the instructions. Once the cakes were
in their pans and safely in the oven, I pointed out to my mother
that it wasn't very hard to do this after all.

My mother, I should add, was a wonderful person, small and childlike, warm and affectionate, and possessed of a wry sense of humor that was shared and appreciated by most everyone in the family. As well, she had a deep love for literature and poetry that she passed to me. Even when I was very young, gifts to me were often books of poetry and novels, Graham Greene and Somerset Maugham. Her volumes of Edna St. Vincent Millay and Robert Frost were lifelong treasures. Bookmarked and annotated in her round handwriting, they had their own bookcase in her room. I often found her there, reading beside the window, which looked out across the meadow behind the house. This was what spoke to her. Duties in the kitchen were uninteresting, even repulsive. She probably regarded food and its preparation as an unwelcome interruption to her poetically inspired reveries. At least, any oncoming mealtime seemed to make her anxious and grumpy, which was not her natural state. As a result, there was a vacancy in our house for someone to prepare a good meal, a role I tried to fill.

Whenever I visited my aunt Peg, it was as if a stuck wheel had been greased and was rolling free at last. Everything flowed. I think I wanted to show my mother that these kitchen adventures could be enjoyable, even fun. And so the birthday cake for Aunt Genee was not only just a way of showing her how much we loved her. It was more than that.

To my everlasting horror, however, the cakes emerged from the oven every bit as flat as they had gone in. They looked like two large chocolate pancakes. My poor mother sensed my disappointment, truly had no idea what to do about all this, and urged me to ice and decorate the unrisen cakes, heavy as lead shields, and serve them to my aunt Genee who acted delighted by the whole thing. I even recall her saying something like "I don't know what you are talking about!" when I made my apology for that flat excuse for a cake.

I must say, the day rather haunted me as a terrific failure. It was years later that I had the revelation about why the cakes had not risen — the baking powder was probably at least ten or more years old. Since she did not cook or, heavens, bake, my mother never used baking powder, which just sat in its colorful tin, pushed aside in the cupboard.

The result of that disappointing day stayed with me. How could baking a cake be that hard, I remember thinking. It was something I was determined to master. That came sooner than I might have thought when cousin George and I discovered something we called Vinegar Cake.

Aside from Julia Child's bible, Aunt Peg had another cookbook, *The I Hate to Cook Book* by Peg Bracken. "Some women, it is said, like to cook. This book is not for them," her book begins. "This book is for those of us who hate to, who have learned, through hard experience, that some activities become no less painful through repetition: childbearing, paying taxes, cooking. This book is for those of us who want to fold our big dishwater hands around a dry martini instead of a wet flounder, come the end of a long day."

I remember feeling confused by this as it seemed like the perfect cookbook for my mother. (In fact, she had a favorite apron emblazoned with the statement: I Hate Housework, given to her by Uncle Jamie one Christmas.) By contrast, my aunt seemed to love to cook; her whole world at times seemed to revolve around it. But the *I Hate to Cook Book* was almost like two sides of her personality: She was very practical and her every day was packed with activities, sometimes making it hard to make something really good for dinner. I think this book appealed to that side of her. There were recipes called Hurry Curry, Fast Rabbit and Bisque Quick.

We loved reading the text out loud. "When you hate to cook, life is full of jolts: for instance, those ubiquitous full-color double-page spreads picturing what to serve on those little evenings when you want to take it easy. You're flabbergasted. You wouldn't cook that much food for a combination Thanksgiving and Irish wake." My aunt and uncle and my cousins and I would read this while we were cooking or maybe while we were washing dishes, which was always a full-family affair. One of us would fling the dish towel onto our shoulder, pick up the book and start reading a favorite passage. And then we'd all have a good laugh.

What was interesting about the book was that it not only dismissed fancy, frou-frou cooking as silly and impractical but more or less proved it by providing recipes that were actually very good. And fast. And easy. This is where we found Vinegar Cake, which, in the book, is called Cockeyed Cake, a chocolate cake that could be mixed and ready for the oven in five minutes. And one of the ingredients was vinegar. Put all the ingredients right in the square pan, beat like crazy and pop it into the oven. It was even faster and less mess than cake mix. Cousin George and I loved this as it was something we could make ourselves when we came in from the outdoors. Hungry? "Let's make Vinegar Cake!" we'd crow. A little more than half an hour later, we were pulling a hot cake out of the oven, pretty proud of ourselves. Sometimes it seemed that the longest part of the whole process was waiting for the cake to cool.

It was not only easy, it was good. Probably because the recipe for that cake resided not in the recipe box but in the beloved Bracken volume, it was not one of the recipes I copied down that day back when Aunt Peg bestowed all those starter recipes on me. I never forgot the cake but was without the recipe. In the meantime, sometime during the 1970s when I was living back to the land, I found what I thought was a recipe even better and almost as easy. It was in a book of favorite New England recipes and was called "Chocolate Pudding." But it wasn't pudding, it was cake, a cake with a lovely center that was more like pudding. The result was a kind of cake with a sauce in the center. Believe me, all my back-to-the-land friends, who also loved their weed, felt this was one of the most divine treats the end of the day could provide.

Vinegar Cake
(from *The I Hate to Cook Book*, with slight alterations)

1½ cups flour

3 tablespoons cocoa

1 teaspoon baking soda

1 cup sugar

½ teaspoon salt

5 tablespoons canola oil

1 tablespoon white vinegar

1 teaspoon vanilla

1 cup cold water

Preheat the oven to 350 degrees. Assemble all the dry ingredients and put them into a greased square (9x9 inch) pan. Make three wells in this mixture: one for the oil, one for the vinegar, one for the vanilla. Add the ingredients to the wells. Pour the cold water over it all. Beat with a fork until it's smooth and you can't see any dry ingredients. Bake at 350 for half an hour. Frost it if you want to but we never did. (Actually, now that I'm older, I prefer to mix everything in a bowl and then scrape the mix into a cake pan. That spoils the spirit of it but mixing in a square pan is awkward.) Serves two hungry cousins.

Chocolate Pudding Cake

3 tablespoons butter

½ cup sugar

1 egg

½ cup milk

2 squares unsweetened chocolate

1 teaspoon baking powder

½ cup flour

pinch of salt

Preheat the oven to 350 degrees. Cream the butter and the sugar. Add the egg and beat. Heat the milk and then melt the chocolate in the milk. Add this to your mixture and then add the dry ingredients. Scrape this into a greased bowl with high, sloping sides. Bake at 350 for 20 minutes. The inside of the cake will be like pudding, the outside will be like cake. Serve hot with whipped cream or ice cream. Serves 6.

As It Should Be

I HOPE I HAVE NOT GIVEN the impression that my uncle was simply a passive observer in my aunt's kitchen, or perhaps a disinterested man, waiting at the table for whatever might be put before him. Quite the contrary, my uncle was perhaps the arbiter of taste around that table and often an active participant in the creation of the family meals. An inch or two shorter than my aunt, Uncle Jamie remained remarkably handsome throughout his life and a man for whom food really mattered. Because he was short, he had to watch his weight, which is something I have always had to do as well, so we formed an early bond in our effort to keep things under control while still enjoying good food. Uncle Jamie was the first man I ever knew to make no bones about the fact that he was on a diet — he would talk about whatever particular regimen he was on with conviction and then, when presented with something irresistible, without apology abruptly abandon all efforts.

One of his passions was dessert and, aside from Orange Marmalade Soufflé, a favorite was Indian pudding. In fact, this was
one of the few foods that was celebrated throughout our family. It
was an essential. At home, we often went out for Sunday dinner
with my grandmother, who was a widow for twenty-five years of
her near-century-long life and eagerly maintained a connection
with my mother and father as well as my sister and me. In order
to be with us as often as she could, she took us out for dinner
after church every Sunday. We had our favorite restaurants and all
of them served Indian pudding. It seems odd to me now that, in
a family that had so little interest in good food, my mother and
my grandmother had opinions about Indian pudding. It had to
be dark. It had to be sweet. It had to be firm, not soupy. A little
sticky, but not too. And it had to be warm. There was a certain
code, almost indecipherable but the outcome was just as it should
be, in the same way my sister and I liked to put a few crystals of
salt on the table while waiting for the waitress to bring our meals.
If we gently leaned the salt shaker against the tiny crystals, we
could make the shaker balance at a slant, almost magically stay-
ing upright. Indian pudding was like that. It had to be just right,
which required a certain peculiar balance.

The further debate was how to finish it off: whipped cream?
Ice cream? Hard sauce? This was one of the very few times my
uncle and I disagreed. He had a real affection for hard sauce and
spent time teaching me how to make it. Just butter and sugar
and brandy. He'd watch me like a hawk when I was trusted to
make it. He especially loved this on his Christmas plum pudding
but he also insisted on it over Indian pudding. For me, for my

grandmother, for my father, even for my mother, it had to be ice cream, melting agreeably over the warm, plump mounds of righteous goodness.

Since there were very few foods that interested my mother, it was one thing that was shared among all of them. Good Indian pudding. I don't actually remember my aunt ever making Indian pudding, which is odd because I remember the debates and the opinions about this classic early American inheritance very well.

Once I was out on my own, I consigned Indian pudding to other rather unfashionable selections. With the rise of *nouvelle cuisine*, Indian pudding became almost permanently detached from the American menu, which is too bad. As with other areas of our heritage, we've lost touch with this basic American food. I certainly abandoned it for quite a while, until I discovered that it was one of those dishes, like baked beans, that was ideal for the wood cookstove. A good Indian pudding needs to cook for at least three hours — some advise as long as six — certainly a fact that probably caused many cooks and certainly virtually all restaurants to give it the heave-ho. Maybe because of its name or its basic ingredients — cornmeal, molasses, milk and eggs — Indian pudding also suffered from an image problem. Calvinistic. Chaste. Dowdy. Very *over.*

But once I set up housekeeping in the woods of New Hampshire back in the 1970s, an act that included the incorporation of a wood cookstove into my kitchen, I took to making Indian pudding. The stove doubled as a heat source and so the oven was ready to receive anything, at any time. The long, slow heat required for this dessert was a perfect match for this early cast-iron appliance.

Some of my friends, when I offered them Indian pudding for dessert, looked as if I had offered them gruel or a bowl of sawdust cereal, which I recall was one friend's comment. Before he had even tasted it. I kind of liked that reaction, as the conversion was therefore all the sweeter. Rarely have I failed to make believers out of these heathens.

My search for a family recipe for Indian pudding was unsuccessful and so I asked my cousins. They offered me the most surprising answer. My aunt found a brand of Indian pudding that was sold in a can. That's right, a *can!* It's hard for me to believe but my cousins jarred my memory — my aunt, when she came down to visit my mother and my grandmother, often brought with her as a house gift, *cans* of Indian pudding, which contained a concoction that they all seemed to think was very good. And available apparently only in New England, which is why Aunt Peg brought it with her on her visits to New Jersey. This revelation was sufficiently deflating that it seemed something akin to finding out that I was really adopted, after all. My cousin also tells me this particular brand of Indian pudding is still available and promises to bring me a can next time I see her. I don't think I could open that can. It would be somehow offensive, heretical to the gospel according to Aunt Peg, an irony I will continue to ponder. Something on par with putting hard sauce on top of this exalted creation, instead of the way it should be, with a slab of vanilla ice cream on top.

Indian Pudding

4 cups milk

⅓ cup cornmeal

1 cup molasses

¼ cup butter

1 teaspoon salt

1 teaspoon ginger

1 egg

In the top of a double boiler, bring the milk to a boil. Whisk in the cornmeal. Cook the mixture for 15 minutes. Add the molasses; stir and cook for five more minutes. Add the rest of the ingredients and pour the batter into a greased baking dish. Bake in a slow oven, 300 degrees for at least three hours. Serves 6.

PART TWO

The Seventies

Dandelion Wine

ON AN OLD PINE SHELF in my basement is a stout brown bottle with a cork in the top. Around the shoulders of the bottle is a soft mantel of dust. If I hold the bottle up to the sun, the light shines through the liquid within, a clear, muted amber. Tilt the bottle, though, and a milky cloud comes up, slow and dreamy, like sediment stirred from the bottom of a deep lake. Our dandelion wine.

There are some things in and about the garden that we do only once. This bottle is there in my cellar to remind me of that. It is probably thirty years now since I made this wine, the first and only time I tried my hand at this art. This was another of those recipes that came to me from my aunt's box of index cards. I wonder now what it was doing among her recipe cards. I have no idea if she ever made it but somehow I think not. Coming on it in the collection, I copied it then because it sounded homey — and country. In spite of the fact that I was settling in the city for the time being, I hoped eventually to make my way to the New England countryside. Dandelion wine. Certainly it was not something I'd ever tasted or perhaps even heard of before. I had no idea what it took to make wine. I imagined stills, such as I had seen in movies about bootlegging, with copper tubing and unusual corks. But also in my mind's eye, I saw fields of dandelions.

One year, in that time of early spring when a sense of renewal stirs in tempo with the sap rising in the trees, I came across that old recipe, which, to date, I had never tried. By that time, I had settled in New Hampshire, where we lived with lush fields all around us. I studied the ingredients listed on the file card. Three pints of dandelion blossoms. An orange. A lemon. A lot of sugar. A little yeast. Those were easy enough to get. And the field at the bottom of our hill would soon be dotted with those bright little yellow beacons of spring. I was living then with my first husband in a house we had built with our own hands, every inch of it. We lived with wood heat and solar hot water. A composting toilet and hand-pumped water. It seems long ago and far away now, but at the time, in the mid-1970s, we loved our freestyle life and shared it with like-minded friends. One of those was Jamie, who lived with her husband in a cabin, much more rustic than ours, in the midst of the great, dense forest that edged our field. Jamie and I, it turned out, would become lifelong friends and she evolved into a well-known artist, creating large, motion-filled impressionist paintings that are admired around the country, but at that time we were new friends. We often shared offbeat recipes for bread and for healing teas brewed from herbs, such as comfrey, which we grew ourselves. My husband and I had a telephone, but Jamie and Bob did not. I waited until the next time I saw her to ask: "Want to make some wine?"

"Do you know how?" she replied.

"I've got a recipe. Dandelion wine," I said. "It sounds easy. It's just dandelions and sugar, mostly."

Within a week or two, when the field was up, new-green and spattered yellow, we went out into it with our pails. We picked just the heads, sunny orbs, free of fragrance. Gripping the blossom between my two forefingers, I'd give a bit of a tug and the flower came free from its tall watery stem, with a tiny audible pop. As we filled the buckets, we pressed down gently, making more room, picked more and pressed down again. Packed down, the blossoms nestled into the bucket like a constellation of little suns. When the buckets were full beyond the possibility of even one more single blossom, they still seemed weightless, like pails full of light.

It was a warm spring day; I can still remember the newly mild air and the naked feeling of happiness that came over me as we picked. The Vietnam war had ended and life seemed easier, mellower. While we picked, we planned the party we would give. The recipe said, "Let stand for two months." By then there would be a harvest, corn on the cob, red ripe tomatoes and raspberry pie. And dandelion wine.

We carried the blossoms back to my house and emptied them into the big ceramic crock that I sometimes used for making pickles or sauerkraut. So today it would be wine. *Pour boiling water over them and let stand three hours.* I stoked the stove with narrow splits of oak and set the big kettle on top of the hottest lid.

We sat at the table beside the kitchen window and got caught up on the news. Winter was always a time when it was harder to get together, the deep snows and the ice keeping us inside our houses. When the water boiled, I poured each of us a mug of tea and then poured the rest over the blossoms. The steaming water passed over them, snuffing their radiance.

Strain and add the sugar. Boil for 30 minutes. My kitchen filled with a curious scent, as if the whole green field and all its tiny flowers were in the pot, sweetened and turned up high. *Slice thin one orange, one lemon and add juice of another lemon. Pour boiling water over the mixture.*

There was more, the cooling off, the adding of the yeast, leaving us plenty of time to talk and drink more tea. The process extended into the evening. Jamie needed to go home. She looked a little worried. "Don't drink it all up on me," she said as she left my wildflower-scented kitchen.

She didn't know, I didn't know, just how unlikely that would be. Before I set the cooling mixture into the basement, where it would sit for two months aging, I spooned a taste. It was something like boiled hay.

At the end of two months, we sampled again. It was almost as bitter. I funneled it into a big old Drambuie bottle we had saved for this moment. The recipe suggested dropping six raisins into the bottom of the bottle so I counted out ten for good measure. *Improves with age!* was the cheery last line on the recipe card.

A few years later, on a cold February afternoon, Jamie came for a visit. We talked for a while over tea. Outside, freezing rain hit against the window. We longed for spring. "Whatever happened to that dandelion wine we made?" she asked, suddenly.

"It's still pretty bitter," I said.

"Can we try it anyway?" she asked.

I brought up the big bottle from the cellar. I took a couple of jelly glasses from the cupboard and ceremoniously poured a bit into each glass. It looked and smelled like liquor, a hopeful sign.

"To spring," I said.

"To spring!" Jamie replied, and we clinked our glasses before taking shy sips.

It seemed just as bitter as it had when I'd spooned from the crock, back when the dandelion blossoms were only a few hours away from their happy spot in the field. We scrunched up our noses.

"Maybe a while longer," she said. And so back down to the shelf it went, back into its place next to the rutabagas.

Every once in a while, we'd check the bottle and it was always bitter and disappointing. Then it was left, forgotten. Jamie and I both divorced and moved to other places, far apart. When I took it off the shelf to move it along with my other belongings, I felt a sense of foolishness, to be carrying this failed experiment elsewhere. But for reasons I couldn't explain, I packed it up and brought it with me into my new life. And there, probably some twenty years later, in yet another cellar, I discovered the old Drambuie bottle, full of memories. I carried it up the stairs, careful not to unsettle the dregs. I uncorked it and, in a slow pour, decanted the golden liquid into a fresh, clean glass bottle. I held it up to the light, remembering the day Jamie and I had picked the dandelions, so long ago in the life of that farm and in our own lives, now so changed. Jamie and I had stayed in touch but there was no more walking through the woods to get caught up on our lives. But that harsh sentence was tempered by the fact that we could talk on the phone all we liked. And get in our cars and arrive to see each other faster than it had taken us to walk through the woods to reach each other's house. When I thought about that, it struck me funny, the tangible evidence of something as astronomically complicated as the theory of relativity, right there in our own complicated lives. I took down a little jigger from the shelf and poured out enough for a taste. The old cellar liquor had a flavor all its own, like sherry or a sweet liqueur — worth savoring. Another complicated theorem surfaced in my mind, the compression of time, a simple, slightly bitter story that had to wait a long time inside a bottle until it had a good ending.

Dandelion Wine

1 quart dandelion blossoms

1½ cups sugar

2 lemons

1 orange

1 tablespoon yeast

6 raisins

Put the blossoms into a large heatproof crock or bowl. Pour 2 quarts of boiling water over them and let stand for 3 hours. Strain then add the sugar. Boil for 30 minutes. Juice one of the lemons and thinly slice the orange and the other lemon and place in the bottom of another heatproof crock or bowl. Pour the boiling mixture over the fruit and let cool. When lukewarm, add the yeast and stir well. Let this stand overnight. In the morning, strain and place in large jar or crock — nothing with a tight cover — and let this stand in a cool, dark place (the cellar is good) for two months. Then bottle it up, placing 6 raisins into each bottle. Cork securely. Improves with age!

(Updated note: We did not think about these things back then, but now it seems necessary to say that these dandelions ought to be gathered from a field that is free of pesticides.)

Bread, Rising

IT WAS BACK IN THOSE DAYS of dandelion wine that I first started to bake bread. My first husband, Michael, worked at a book manufacturing plant in Brattleboro, Vermont. He often came home with books that were right off the press. Even the editors hadn't seen them yet. A lifelong book lover, I regarded these offerings like newly minted money. Or better. Novels not yet reviewed and new writings by some of my favorite writers rose up beside my bedside.

One night Michael came home with *The Complete Book of Breads* by Bernard Clayton, Jr. I remember staring at the jacket photo for a long time, studying the breads that rested there, an assortment of loaves, round and oblong, braided and flat, beautifully browned, each loaf a different shade, all nestled into what looked like an adobe oven. In the foreground a bowl of rising dough, a golden color, was surrounded by dark spices, brown eggs and whole-grain flours. Regarding this luscious display, I suddenly wondered if I could ever make bread.

I grew up outside New York City, a member of the baby-boomer generation, the first generation to think that chicken came onto the planet in cellophane-wrapped packages and that bread was made in big factories with fragrant smokestacks. The idea of making one's own bread represented a kind of kitchen watershed, a goal that seemed out of my reach. The aroma of home-baked bread certainly was not anything I ever experienced in my house growing up, nor do I recall any of my aunts or grandmothers baking bread, not even my beloved Massachusetts aunt Peg. I think that Bernard Clayton's also might have been the first cookbook I ever read, cover to cover, underlining sentences as if it were a textbook, which, I eventually realized, it was.

I also scrutinized the photo of Mr. Clayton on the jacket flap. Except for the apron, he looked like a businessman, the kind of white-collar fellow we of that generation enjoyed dismissing. He was from the Midwest. According to the flap copy, he had worked in journalism and public relations and at a university. Bread baking was his hobby and in the dedication, he thanked his wife for letting him use her kitchen. Nevertheless, his careful prose and fastidious instructions won my complete respect. Interesting and sometimes witty commentary prefaced just about every recipe and provided a gauge by which one might judge the feasibility of each recipe. When I had absorbed as much as I could from the reading of that book, I scanned the recipes looking for ones that he thought were simple, starting with the Thirty-

Minute White Bread and the Instant Blend Buttermilk Bread ("easy to make") and went shopping for the ingredients. It's hard to recall or know what I might have done wrong with those first few tries but the results of my efforts turned into hard lumps of dough that I eventually hurled into the compost in utter frustration. Why I persisted is curious. Maybe it was that alluring photo on the cover of the book. But after what seems like quite a few failed efforts, a domed loaf, brown and fragrant, came forth from my oven. The loaf lasted less than a day, as I sliced it and buttered it and ate it, and then tried it all over again, like a hungry traveler home from a hike. Only I had been nowhere but in the kitchen, working the dough, kneading it on the board, learning what good dough feels like in my hands. "Push, turn, fold," Clayton instructed and I followed. He urged his readers to pummel and punch, and it seemed to be good therapy, a chance to let some of those frustrations out on the dough and create something good at the same time. He even encouraged a method of lifting the dough above the head and crashing it down onto the counter. I seemed to love that permission.

I discovered that if Neil Young or Jackson Browne was cranked up on the stereo while I kneaded, the dough responded. I punched and jabbed and then lifted and smacked it down. A rhythm developed that seemed part of the process. Eventually, I knew when a dough was alive and when it was dead. Good dough almost breathed back at me. It almost had a pulse. Over time, my technique improved. I tested the temperament of the dough, even learned how to resuscitate a batch near death. Michael was as enthusiastic as I was, maybe more so. He took the bread to work and bragged about it to his friends. They wanted me to make loaves for them, as well, and so I started taking orders. Just like that, I was in business.

By that time I had tried virtually every recipe in the book, the Rich White Bread and the Feather Bread, the English Muffin Bread, the Russian Black Bread and the Anadama Bread. These loaves emerged from my oven, week after week, as I progressed through the almost five hundred pages of recipes and bread-baking advice. I learned about yeast and sourdough starters (which, for years, I kept in a little crock on the kitchen counter), about flours and about what different ingredients like sugar or butter do to a bread dough. Bernard Clayton guided me from afar, from his cosmopolitan, debonair kitchen in Missouri to my simple, antiquated New Hampshire farmhouse. Bread baking became our imaginary bond.

The rising became my favorite part in the process. It's the original double or nothing. These miraculous events don't come easy, though. I had already fended off some folklore I'd picked up along the way, such as the idea that one should never bake bread on rainy days, because of the low atmospheric pressure that would hinder the rising process. I couldn't afford to follow that advice because I was making bread every day. And, it occurred to me, anyone who is baking bread for sale has to get the process going no matter what the weather is outdoors. So I eventually let go of my anxiety when baking on a foul-weather day (though I did notice that it doesn't rise *as well*). But I did find that one needs to find a warm place to ensure the magical levitation. "No drafts," Clayton cautioned. I found out he was dead right about that.

A warm place was relatively easy to find in our house as we had two woodstoves and so one or the other usually had a nice warm periphery but the part about it being draft free was another matter. At that time, we were living in a rented farmhouse, very old and very drafty. So I made little partitions to keep the drafts away and never set it near any of the many doors in that house.

When ready to rise, the dough is something like a small bundle of life. It's heavy yet buoyant and expectant. Put your finger against the skin and it springs back in reply. I enjoyed tucking the yeasty being into the nicely greased bowl and covering that with a clean towel. I'd set it beside the stove and in an hour, under the cloth, the dough had expanded, an instant pregnancy.

As I went along, I marked the book as if it were a notebook. Next to the Whole Wheat Bread, I put a star, but next to the Buttermilk Whole Wheat Bread, I wrote, "not so good." The Sour Cream Rye Bread "did not rise." I experimented with the recipes in the book, trying baguettes and then sweet breads, whole grains and whites. For my customers, I made one of the white bread recipes every morning — that seemed to be the most popular — and then I chose another whole-grain alternative.

It was hard to figure out how much to charge but I settled on seventy-five cents a loaf, which was a bit higher than the going rate in the early 1970s. I couldn't imagine charging a dollar. My little enterprise was popular. I got up very early every morning so that the bread was just coming out of the oven as Michael was leaving for work at 8 A.M. I sent him off with a sack of fresh bread each morning and in turn he came home with cash that we stashed in a bean pot on the kitchen counter. We were saving so we could build our own house and we believed that by building that house, we could live self-sufficiently. So this bread-baking venture seemed like a good start and a path to the future.

But after a while, I realized I wasn't really making any money. Most of what I was taking in went toward the purchase of ingredients. Everyone loved the bread and orders increased but it was a break-even proposition. At that time people, including myself, were resistant to paying more than a dollar for a loaf of bread. It seemed unthinkable. Michael and I thought about buying an industrial oven and we thought about purchasing bulk ingredients but neither seemed practical and both were, basically, beyond our means. So I stopped baking bread to sell and I took a job at the printing company, proofreading galleys. It was an easier way to make the money we needed to build that house. Soon after that, new bakeries sprang up around us, mostly started by folks like ourselves, who were looking to live what was then known as "the good life," a concept promoted by Helen and Scott Nearing, Vermont back-to-the-landers whose book *Living the Good Life* we had studied almost as hard as I had studied the bread book.

Though I no longer sold loaves, baking bread did not leave my life entirely. One of my favorite recipes became the gift I gave for Christmas each year. I loved making Christmas Braid, a recipe I had found in a newspaper and adapted according to Clayton. It had a subtle sweetness enhanced by raisins. I taught myself to make tight braids, which were tricky as they tended to unfurl once the rising began, or open during the baking process. I was also proud of the egg glazing that I had worked on so that the loaves had an even, honey-colored sheen to them. After they'd cooled on the racks, I wrapped each loaf in foil, tied them all with ribbons and made a Christmas Eve round in my car, the back seat stacked with fresh loaves to deliver to loved ones. Each year, I baked more and more of these loaves as my gift list grew. And I always baked two extra loaves to put into the freezer for special times later on.

One year, the power failed during a cold snap. I set the contents of the freezer outside in a cooler to keep it all frozen. Not everything fit so I put the bread loaves, the least dear of our hoardings, on top of the cooler. It was very cold out so I knew they would stay frozen. In the morning, the loaves were gone. I could see a trail of prints fading off into the woods. I was surprised and sorrowful since we always looked forward to bringing those loaves out, sometime in February. I wondered what critter was enjoying our beloved braids.

One morning in the spring, when all had thawed, I opened the back door and found one of the loaves on the doorstep, foil wrap tight and undisturbed. I couldn't imagine how the Christmas Braid had not only survived the winter but had returned. The next morning, I caught my hound dog in the act of returning the second loaf. She was crossing the field, carrying the foil-wrapped treasure gingerly in her mouth. She dropped it at my feet and looked at me with pride. All I can figure is that, back on that cold winter night, she ran off with the breads and buried them somewhere in the snow. And when the thaw came, she unearthed them and brought them back. Unlikely, and yet the only explanation I've ever been able to make for the return of those stolen loaves, which betrayed nothing of the winter they spent buried in the woods. And, yes, we ate them. If anything, they were better than any we'd ever had.

For some time, I stopped baking bread altogether. Like everyone else, I found it was time-consuming and artisan bakeries that made good wholesome loaves sprouted everywhere. But then I discovered that I missed it, not just the bread but the whole process. Now I bake bread from time to time, always with a great deal of pleasure, feeling confident in my touch. The dough springs lightly under my hands as I work it on the countertop. I punch and pummel and lift up the mass and slam it back down, as effective as any primal scream. It all makes me smile for those old days. Bernard Clayton's masterpiece, stained and worn as it is, remains prominent on my kitchen shelf. While I work, even though the house is silent, I can hear Neil Young singing "Long May You Run." *We've been through some things together. With trunks of memories still to come. We found things to do in stormy weather. Long may you run.*

When the dough is plump and lively, I set the promising mass in a clean bowl and put it in a warm, protected place knowing that within an hour, I will have twice what I have now, the small miracle of the bread of life.

Christmas Braid

2 cups milk, scalded

1 cup water

1 cup sugar

2 tablespoons (2 packages) yeast

2 teaspoons salt

12+ cups flour

1 teaspoon grated lemon peel

5 tablespoons butter, melted

2 eggs

¼ cup raisins

Scald the milk and water. Let cool to body temperature — test it on your wrist as you would a baby's bottle. Add the sugar, yeast, and salt to the liquid. Add about 2-3 cups of flour along with the lemon peel, melted butter, eggs and raisins. Gradually work the rest of the flour in, a cup at a time, until the mixture is no longer sticky. You may need more or less than 12 cups. Place the dough in an oiled bowl. Cover and let stand in warm spot until doubled.

When it's doubled, punch it down. Decide how many loaves you would like to make. There is enough dough to make six small loaves but you may want to make only three large ones. Or one super large loaf. Depending on how many loaves you decide to make, divide the dough into that many parts. Then divide each lump into three equal parts and roll each part between your hands until they are long thin ropes of equal length. Place the three ropes beside each other, secure the tops to each other and then braid, careful to make each section equal to the other. When you get to the end, seal the ends together much the same as you did at the top. Wet your hands if need be as water can help make a good seal.

Remember that the braids have to withstand another rising and then the baking process and if the braids are not well bonded, the strands will separate and not bake as one loaf. Preheat the oven to 375 degrees. When you're happy with your braids, set them on an ungreased cookie sheet and place them in a warm place to rise again. When they've risen, brush the loaves with egg wash (slightly beaten egg whites — use two for this recipe) and bake for 35 to 45 minutes.

A Kitchen for Life

IN THE HOME that we eventually built with the money saved from various jobs (including not only baking bread but also picking asparagus, proofreading galleys and selling composting toilets) was the kitchen that Michael and I designed together. We built the house in the summer of 1976 with money saved and no money borrowed. "Pay as you go!" Scott Nearing thundered into the microphone at a lecture we attended and we tried to live by his maxim. We designed the house ourselves, a simple Cape with a center chimney, two bedrooms upstairs under the eaves and downstairs, a big living room and an open kitchen with plenty of room for a big country table beside the wide, south-facing window.

The center of that house was not so much the chimney (which had four flues and a copper hatch that allowed us to clean the chimney without having to climb up the roof on a ladder) but the stoves attached to it. In spite of my love for fireplaces, greatly fostered by memories of my aunt and uncle's warm hearth, we discarded the notion of a fireplace as expensive and inefficient, complicated to build, an important consideration since we were to do all the masonry ourselves. Stoves would give, and keep, more heat, which was the purpose to begin with. So we had a Norwegian box stove in the living room and a Glenwood cast-iron wood cookstove for the kitchen.

To my eyes, the stove we had chosen, a Glenwood C, was the perfect marriage of form and function. The black surface of the cast iron, smooth as stone, the ornate corners and Victorian flourishes, the homely curl of the short but rugged legs, the gleam of the chrome trim, all these features manifested a certain grace and comfort. The very presence of the stove seemed to communicate a confidence that, no matter what, something good would come from this thing of beauty. At the same time, the complicated engineering of the oven drafts, which directed the path of the flames around the oven box or straight up the chimney, and the sensible features such as the oven door pedal, which enabled the cook to use her foot to open the door when her hands were full, and the detachable trivets that swiveled and added variable warming surfaces, all these things, small and large, contributed to the feeling that this, *this*, was a giant of design and engineering.

Of course, at first, I had no idea how ingenious these inventions were. I was to experience a baptism by fire. This stove was to become the center of our house, provider of heat and good food. But before it could earn such an important distinction, I needed to learn to cook on it and in it.

In the bookstore in Brattleboro, I found a cookbook with an alluring photo of a similar old black beauty on the cover. But that turned out to be just that — an alluring photo. Inside there were no recipes or instructions for this old way of cooking. Pretty soon, after a thorough search, I discovered that I was on my own for this voyage of discovery. I knew of no one who had ever cooked on a woodburning cookstove.

My first attempt to bake chicken was an indication of how far I had to go. After seven hours, the little pieces of meat inside that oven had a pale, deathly pallor. They were warm and beaded with sweat, as if they'd been through an ordeal, but not really even hot. Quite a few further attempts ended up in the garbage before I discovered the proper dampers to close to keep the heat in the oven. The stove itself was in great shape. It had belonged to an old woman in Brattleboro who had kept the iron polished and the nickel bright. From what I know now, if the old cast-iron stoves are well cared for, they will last virtually forever. The only way to destroy them is to consciously do so. At that time, people were taking stoves like that out to the back field and busting them up with sledge hammers. They were big and heavy and took up valuable space in the house or the shed. They had no value, not even as scrap metal, and only a few scattered crazy hippies were interested in resurrecting them.

After the first few months of trial and error, I became a believer as I learned the way these stoves worked. I could fine-tune the surface heat by sliding pots from one side of the stove to the other — one side would produce a boil, the middle a simmer, and the far right would just keep something hot. And there were several shelves and trivets on which I could keep things like bread or muffins warm.

At flea markets, I collected cast-iron skillets of all sizes and any kind of cookware made of cast iron. I tried to find pieces that had not lost their seasoning, which is to say, their smooth cooking surface. Once a piece becomes rusty, it's hard to regain the perfect smoothness that cast iron can hold, like the stoves, if taken care of. A well-seasoned skillet is almost like Teflon, as it hardly needs greasing to be able to slide omelets or pancakes off their surface with just a nudge of a spatula.

It wasn't long before I became the local evangelist for what almost amounted to a cooking religion. At a time in the early 1970s when this country was enduring the first of its many "energy crises," I believed with all my heart and soul in cooking with wood. The whole concept made so much sense to me, the big black heart pumped heat into the house and at the same time provided a constant flame for cooking anything, any time of day or night. The fuel was collected from our own back yard, not half-way around the world where wars were erupting over oil. The only key to these stoves was that you had to be there and that fit with our philosophy of providing for ourselves. By then, Michael had abandoned the book business (most of it was leaving Brattleboro anyway) and turned to carpentry. Once people saw our house, so simple yet ingenious in design and so sturdy in construction, they asked him to build them one "just like it." And he did, one, two, three, that sweetly designed house began to appear elsewhere in the region and Michael, it turned out, had taken up his hammer and tools for the rest of his working life. And I was expanding my business of freelance editing and writing. Every once in a while, I would take off my jeans, spruce myself up and drive in to Boston to meet with the editors and publishers who were giving me work. I'm sure they had no idea that my work took place in a sun-powered, wood-heated home with a composting toilet, set in the bosky woods of a still-innocent New Hampshire.

Aside from that exalted stove, the kitchen in that house was designed almost organically. We worked with the space that we had and tried to create a useful working area surrounding the stove. I had a theory about kitchens, that the overhead cabinets so common in suburban kitchens were ugly and inconvenient. I believed in pantries for they hide nothing and make it easy to find whatever you need with one sweeping glance. I also wanted open shelves. They were a lot less expensive than the cabinets and they allowed me to display the small collection of yellowware I was acquiring at auctions and sales. I wanted the bowls and pitchers, which I could pick up for a dollar or two, to be visible, to show them off, because, like the stove, I loved their designs, quirky and mirthful, and their bright yellows, blues and reds that gave the room color without paint. For me, all of this had a powerful, comforting nostalgia — oddly a nostalgia for an era I had never experienced. In all, the kitchen was designed for practicality, and for beauty. We found an old enamel sink — no chips! — as well as a claw-foot tub for the bathroom. We were able to get both for free since, at that time, these items were regarded by others in the same way as the cookstove — outdated and suitable only for the field behind the house or for the dump.

The other item that made the kitchen completely functional was a Hoosier cabinet. In the 1930s, this was a brand of furniture and a design for a kitchen cabinet that could, if arranged properly, store everything a cook would need inside her kitchen. The dishes and glasses. The pots and pans. The flour and the potatoes. Everything. All in one cabinet. I started looking around for one and found them at auctions and in antique stores, but they were expensive.

Every time I went to get raw milk from the farm at the end of the road, I saw what I wanted: a beautiful Hoosier cabinet, outside the milk room, currently being used by that farmer to store paints. I approached him one day and offered to trade him metal shelving for the Hoosier. He gave a kind of shrug and said, "Sounds good." And so I had my Hoosier, which, when stripped and refinished, had a beautiful mellow sheen to it. To this day, this ingeniously designed cabinet holds all the things a kitchen needs.

The result of all of this was simple but beautiful. We made the open shelves and the kitchen counter out of local pine, smoothly planed and coated with multiple layers of polyurethane. In the center of the countertop, Michael set a large piece of marble — another scavenging find — so I could knead the bread dough in style. He made drawers and where there were openings, such as under the sink, we hung curtains that I made from colorful cloth.

The interesting thing about this kitchen is that, as my life has unfolded, I have moved several times, always ever after to an old house, not a new one, and yet, in the process, I've created three more kitchens and they all, basically, follow this same pattern.

Open shelves, an ample pantry, a cookstove, and the old-style sink. Along the way, a gas stove, circa 1930, has been added as a partner to the woodstove and an essential for summer cooking. My collection of pitchers and bowls has stayed with me wherever I've gone and I still cook on that cookstove. I don't proselytize anymore. I realize this, what amounts to a lifestyle, is not for everyone but I'll work with this stove until I can't feed the wood into it any longer — hopefully for a very long time.

German Apple Pancake

This is my favorite recipe to make on the cookstove. That the skillet is all cast iron, with no wooden or plastic handles, allows you heat it up on the stovetop for the first part of the recipe and then pop it into the oven for the second stage. This works with a gas or electric stove as well as the wood-fired cookstove. You will need to have two skillets for this recipe.

   3 large eggs
   ¾ cup milk
   ¾ cup flour
   ½ teaspoon salt
   1 tablespoon butter

FILLING:
4 large, tart apples (Choose an apple that will stay firm. McIntosh
      apples become mushy. I like Macoun, but Granny Smiths are
      good, too.)
2 tablespoons melted butter

¼ cup sugar

1 teaspoon cinnamon

Preheat the oven to 450 degrees. In the blender, whip the eggs, milk, flour and salt until nice and smooth. In a heavy, 9-inch iron skillet, melt the butter and run it around the edges to make sure the bottom and sides of the pan are well coated. As soon as it's really hot, pour in the batter and put the skillet into the oven. After 15 minutes, lower the oven to 350 degrees. The pancake will puff and bubble, resembling a hilly terrain. If it puffs too much, prick it with a fork to tame it. Continue baking for another 10 minutes.

While the pancake is baking, prepare the apple filling. Peel and slice the apples as you would for a pie. In another heavy skillet of similar size, sauté the apple slices in the butter and add the sugar and cinnamon. Cook for 8 to 10 minutes over a medium flame. The apples should be tender but not mushy. When the pancake is slightly browned on top, slide it onto a platter and pour the apple filling over the top. Serve at once, cutting it in wedges like a pie. This can be served for breakfast or as a dessert. If you serve it for dessert, a little ice cream or whipped cream doesn't hurt. Serves 4.

The Chicken and the Egg

THE FIRST CHICKENS we raised were for the eggs. We ordered a batch of chicks from Sears and they came to us through the mail in a box. At that time, in the spring, our post office was often alive with cheeping sounds as everyone was getting their new chicks to be raised either for eggs or for meat. Who cannot love a little chick, all soft yellow fuzz, powered strictly by anxiety? They were like an Easter display come to life. We set up an incubator for them in a washtub nestled with a bed of hay and warmed by a lightbulb that hung close to the bed — all this under instructions from Marge and Skip, our inspirations.

I met Marge at the printing company where I worked. I was a proofreader and she worked in the bindery. She was in her late sixties then, I would guess, a widow who lived with her bachelor son, Skip. I passed by their house on my way home and often I gave her a ride home when we got off the seven o'clock shift. Our conversations offered a wealth of information for me. She had been born in the house where she was still living. Their garden was rich with the leavings of many generations of pigs and chickens. Once, to our surprise, Marge and Skip knocked on our door on a Sunday afternoon bearing a pound of fresh-cured bacon and a dozen double-yolkers. It was the first time I'd ever heard of a double-yolker — just what it sounds like, an egg with two yolks — and that a dozen could be gathered in a relatively short time seemed remarkable to me. And they had cured the bacon in their own smokehouse, a small shed behind their house. From then on, in spite of our differences, Marge and Skip and Michael and I were fast friends. I gave Marge rides and they returned the favor with bread and eggs and tips on small farming. We soaked it all up like warm sunshine.

It seems I could reach back and pull up an entire encyclopedia of things that Marge and Skip taught us. So much of what motivated us to become self-sufficient was fueled by our outrage at the proliferation of nuclear power plants, one of which was nearby in Vernon, Vermont, and another about to be built in Seabrook, New Hampshire. What was serendipitous was that Marge and Skip's way of life, which was simply sensible, gave us many tools toward our goal of self-sufficiency. Marge and Skip and the thousands like them in the hills all around us had no particular opinion about nuclear power and understood little about it. They were still grateful for the conveniences electricity had brought them and seemed confused when we talked about living without electricity. We did not want to be connected to the grid that was feeding off foreign oil and posing health threats to those who lived near it. My old Volkswagen bore only one bumper sticker: Split Wood Not

Atoms. We believed that everyone would be much better off if we could provide our own resources to heat our houses and leave the sheiks out of the equation. Similarly, we felt it did not make sense to import produce from halfway around the world when we could grow our own food in our own New Hampshire soil and handle it in our own hands. We had lessons to learn along the way and ironically, Marge and Skip showed us part of the way.

Marge and Skip gave us our first rooster — he was old and they no longer wanted to feed him. They said we could kill him for meat. The rooster was going to die anyway and the economy of the act appealed to our newfound sense of country logic. With their guidance, we killed him and dressed him and I baked him in the oven. But the meat was tough and the experience was unpleasant. We thought maybe we should stick to eggs. They encouraged us to get a pig and told us how simple it would be for us to make a smokehouse, where we could cure bacon and hams. We thought about that, but we wanted chickens first. With their counsel, we bought our first flock of laying hens, Golden Comets, still the prettiest hens I've ever seen.

We had a big old barn but it was all big spaces with no good access to the outdoors. So we made a smaller pen in the underside of the barn, with a sweet little ramp the hens could walk down into the fenced-in yard we made for them. We cut pole-sized trees for fence posts and set them into the rocky ground. Then we tucked chicken wire underground to prevent night (or day) marauders from visiting and digging a subterranean entrance under the fence.

I loved "the ladies," as we called them. We had about twenty of them and when they got old enough to produce eggs, we were once again in business with Michael's co-workers. We kept a yellow plastic bucket beside the kitchen door and first thing every morning, I'd head to the henhouse, grabbing the bucket on my way out. Even though we made nests for them, they seemed to lay wherever they wanted to. "Morning, ladies!" I'd croon as I crouched down into the little pen, which was just four feet high, ducking and waddling around in a squat, rummaging in the hay and out in the yard, filling the little bucket with new eggs.

Back inside the house, I'd unpack the bucket onto the kitchen counter. The eggs were every lovely shade of brown you can think of — cocoa, café au lait, cinnamon, beige, almond, oatmeal. I liked to keep them in a bowl on the counter to show off their subtle, earthy colors. I'd scrub each one with a brush under the running faucet, washing off bits of hay and manure, appreciating for the first time in my life what a fabulous package the egg is, how perfectly hardy and yet delicate the shell is, how beautifully shaped, how amazingly contained is this perfect food inside the package, the clear white and its brilliant yellow center. While I washed, I contemplated the idea of perfection. I never thought an egg would take me to such places.

Until I'd eaten a truly fresh egg, I never even really liked them. I learned, somewhere along the way, that most of the eggs we buy in the store are as much as a month or two old. Well, not these. As I brushed them, I packed them into egg boxes I'd saved and every few days packed several dozen into a bag for Michael to take to work with him. His co-workers paid seventy-five cents a dozen, which helped pay for the feed.

We hooked up a wide Venezuelan hammock to the big beams underneath the barn, right next to the henhouse. On hot summer afternoons, we'd sometimes climb into the hammock and lie still. The hens cooed and moaned and hummed while they pecked in the yard, sounds that I found meditative and soothing.

But all about the chickens was not soothing. As is the case on all farms, there are jolts. Eventually, we bought a rooster for our ladies, as we thought it would be great to raise our own chicks from the eggs laid here, rather than sending away for new chicks every spring. I had also read that fertilized eggs are more nutritious for you. And, last but not least, the presence of the rooster would, we thought, keep the ladies happy. We always tend to insert our own feelings into our animals' lives, which seems to be a consistent error. Dogs, for instance, don't really want to wear coats. It's our imagination that makes us think they need them, as we do. They already have coats and the application of a woolen garment is irritating to dogs. But, we do these things and so we thought a rooster with our hens would make everyone happy. Well, no doubt it made the rooster happy as he went about, applying his manhood to each and every startled lady in the yard. Feathers flew and that contented cooing became shrieks of outrage.

But then we found that we had broody hens, keeping the fertilized eggs warm and, we hoped, eventually hatching them. So that seemed like success, of sorts. We were admittedly new at this so we made mistakes. One morning, Michael went out to gather the eggs. It was important to remember which hens were brooding and which ones weren't but he apparently forgot. Or at least that's what we think must have happened as he brought in a bucket of eggs and I took a couple from the top of the bucket and prepared to make a scrambled breakfast. This will live with me forever, as I cracked the egg on the edge of the bowl and opened the shell, which revealed a nearly fully formed chick, covered with soft red fuzz, ready to be hatched.

No eggs were eaten that morning.

That first rooster also became a hunted man because he was so disagreeable that he often went after us when we came in to collect eggs. One morning he came at Michael, aimed his spur and drove it right through Michael's boot. This was war. We tried to catch him but he was elusive as a frog in water. Michael, not to be outdone by a rooster, went inside and got his revolver, came out and began shooting at the rooster. I hid inside, totally hor-rified at both these violent acts. Michael came back frustrated. "Couldn't get the fucker," he muttered. "I fired the whole round." I said nothing. But, eventually, we did get him and readied him for the pot. When we butchered him, his intestines were full of brass casings from Michael's bullets. Roosters like shiny objects and he'd ingested all of them, the remains of what had been meant to terminate him.

Another time, we found that egg production had gone down. We couldn't figure out why. What had happened that our hens were not producing? Our egg business fell off sharply. One morning, I noticed a groove in the nest where one of our broody hens had been sitting. It was smooth as if something had packed it down. It took a while but eventually we connected the very large black snake that sunned itself on the big stone foundation of the south end of the barn with the vanishing eggs. Michael observed him one evening, slithering up through the floorboards, into the hen house, and up into that nest. While our apparently clueless lady sat still, he stole in underneath her, unhinged his jaw, stealthily took in whatever eggs were in the nest, and slithered back down. Somehow Michael solved that problem. I maybe didn't want to know how.

As well, we decided at last to escalate our enterprise and raise chickens for meat. Again, we wanted to take responsibility for what we ate so we reasoned that if we were going to eat meat, we ought to make it our own, which included raising it and butchering it ourselves. Thinking we would be better off if we raised a lot at once and got the unpleasant task over with, we bought a hundred leghorns, best for meat. They raised up in six weeks. Ignorant then of the growth hormones added to feed, I was amazed how fast they grew. But when the time came to slaughter them all, we were faced with a grueling, dawn to dusk task that left us exhausted, blood-spattered and despondent at what we had done. I don't recall what we did with all the coolers filled with the fresh chicken gleaned over the course of that long day but I know we never ate it. The smell of blood and scalded feathers lingered in the air, I swear, for years to come. In fact, it was a very long time before we ate meat of any kind after that.

Even in spite of all the eggs we sold, we had eggs galore, which called upon me to find a variety of ways to use them. Angel food cake, which calls for a dozen whites, was a favorite as were Belgian waffles and soufflés, which were sometimes temperamental and fussy. I dug back to the packet of recipe cards from Aunt Peg. Her recipe for Cheese Strata became a favorite for its impressive rise — like a soufflé but without the work — and for its wonderful flavor.

During those years, we had several flocks of Golden Comets, as well as Rhode Island Reds. Once Michael and I parted, chickens left my life. Sadly. I often entertain the fantasy of having chickens again, a little flock of laying hens that could peck and scratch in the yard and, at night, coo and bawk and flap inside the barn. Oh, yes, I'd love to have chickens in my life again. But just for the eggs, and no roosters this time.

Cheese Strata

For years, while we were vegetarians, we ate this at least once a week. I have experimented over the years with all kinds of bread, trying whole grain as well but this recipe really comes out best when you use a standard white bread. Aunt Peg always used Pepperidge Farm. Whatever bread you choose, it's easy, cheap and delicious. Oh, and nutritious, too.

12 slices of day-old bread
½ pound cheddar cheese, grated
4 eggs
2½ cups milk
1 teaspoon dry mustard
1 tablespoon chopped onion
1 teaspoon salt
fresh ground pepper

Arrange 6 slices of bread in the bottom of the lightly greased baking dish. A 9x13 or a 2-quart dish is adequate for this recipe. Cover with half the cheese and then with the remaining slices of bread. In the blender, whirl all the rest of the ingredients. Pour this over the bread and cheese. Let this stand, covered, at least an hour. I sometimes make this up in the morning and put it in the fridge before going off to work. After work, I pop it into the oven. Bake, uncovered, at 350 degrees for one hour. Serves 6.

Pizza on the Porch

THERE WERE A FEW YEARS there in the 1970s when we provided for ourselves virtually everything we ate. At that time, we had an active root cellar, which was nothing more than the cellar of the house, but the important thing was that it had a dirt floor and, since there was no furnace running, the temperature remained constant in the winter at about thirty-five to forty degrees — the perfect keeping environment. In fact, for the years we lived without electricity, the cellar served as our refrigerator.

Down there were crocks of pickles and vats of sauerkraut, boxes of beets and carrots and potatoes and onions, all pulled from our big garden in the fall, and apples from our trees and from our neighbor's trees — any trees we could find that had not been sprayed with pesticides — and shelves lined with Mason jars filled with pears and piccalilli and tomatoes. Most of all, tomatoes. For a number of years, every fall I put up something like eighty-four quarts of tomatoes, which I had somehow calculated was two quarts a week, which did not include the summer months, when we were harvesting fresh tomatoes. I believe we planted two dozen tomato plants in anticipation of that kind of harvest — which also included a healthy consumption of tomatoes for the table throughout the late summer months. In the winter, using this cellar bounty, we ate stir-fried vegetables with rice and a lot of spaghetti. But what we really craved was pizza.

When we moved north from Philadelphia in 1973, one of the things Michael and I missed most was a good pizza. It simply was not available in our part of New England. There might have been one or two places that served "pizza" but it always turned out to be a frozen pizza or something equally unpalatable. Perhaps those early years spurred me to greater culinary heights by the simple maxim, if you cannot buy it, make it yourself. If I thought of bread as a challenge, pizza certainly was the grail. In his big tome of recipes, Bernard Clayton did not have a single recipe for pizza dough, which I suppose is not, technically, a bread. Still, it was the first time he had failed me. I started to search for a recipe for pizza dough. In the meantime, we learned to get along without the pie. When we went home to visit our parents (Michael's were on Long Island, mine in New Jersey), we always brought home bags of bagels (another thing that was impossible to find north of White Plains), a sack of fresh steamer clams, and a pizza from a particular parlor near Michael's home on Long Island. But we rarely went down there, so it was a long famine between feasts.

Pizza was not, by any means, a family tradition from my past. My father was of English heritage and thought anything of foreign name or extraction suspect. Not only was everything we ate somewhat bland and without much variety, it was of recognizable ingredients. Chicken. Potato. Spinach. If he ever said the name, which was very rare, he pronounced it *PIE-zah*. And he apparently had no interest in trying one. To be fair, the American menu of the 1950s and early 60s was hardly as international as it is now. Therefore, the first pizza I ever encountered was during my freshman year in college, at a pizza place outside Philadelphia. I thought I'd never tasted anything so good and, of course, regarded it as something that was purchased in a flat cardboard box, not something one made oneself. Like most everyone else, I felt that to be able to make pizza, you had to be Italian, wear a chef's hat, and be able to spin the dough like a top at the end of your finger.

The first pizza recipe I found used a biscuit crust. This was OK, better than anything we could buy at the take-out but it wasn't really very good. The tomato sauce somehow made the crust soggy and only the corner pieces were rigid enough to pick up and eat with one hand, the sign of a good pie. And, of course, the flavor wasn't right. I finally found, in a newspaper, a recipe for a pie dough using yeast. I set to it. It wasn't bad! Since I didn't have a circular pizza pie pan and had no idea where I might find something like that, I used my cookie sheet and made rectangular pies. Just as good. Pizzas started coming out of my wood-fired oven more and more frequently and the result improved. I discovered I could put just about anything on them, peppers and onions, mushrooms, garlic, whatever was in the house. And I had all those quarts of tomatoes in the cellar, which I would simmer down to a thick sauce before pouring that onto the risen crust.

I was determined to make good pie, which was Michael's term for pizza. Eventually, I came across a recipe in the *Christian Science Monitor* for pizza on the grill. This intrigued me. Because of our unusual cooking facilities, we often made dinner on the outdoor grill, since firing up the oven in the summertime was a hot enterprise. The recipe included cornmeal and whole wheat flour. I tried it and thought the result was extraordinary except that the bread was more like flatbread than pizza dough. For flatbreads, I loved this recipe, but it wasn't what I liked for pizza. I decided to change it around a little and make it the way I would for regular pizza, baked in the oven, to see how it would come out. On the very first try, I knew that this was the recipe I'd been looking for. I eventually eliminated the whole wheat flour but the addition of the cornmeal gave it body and texture. Adapted, I have used this recipe ever since with consistently good results.

One summer, some friends from the city called to invite themselves for the weekend. We loved it when our friends came because they were all, every one of them, skeptical of life in the country. "What do you do for fun?" they would ask, as if we were living in a barren landscape devoid of culture. "Do you ever get to see any movies?" they persisted. What did they think, civilization ended at the New Hampshire border?

Truthfully, though, when we first moved here, it had been hard to answer those questions since we were in the midst of severe culture shock. Jobs were scarce and pay scales were very low. There were many things that seemed unusually slow and backward to us. Everything we had expected had not turned out to be everything we wanted. We wondered if we had made a mistake and occasionally pondered returning to the city. But the proximity to big forests and fragrant farmland was like a balm to all the fractures of the city: the search for a parking place, the many locks necessary to safeguard one's dwelling, the fear of walking alone at night in certain places. And at that particular time in 1973, monstrously long lines at the city gas pumps. It all had had a corrosive effect. It was hard to explain to our friends the sense of freedom we felt. A liberation, and, even further, a whole new life. But there were lingering issues. One of the things I remember most was the lack of ethnic diversity. At that time in northern New England, there were very few blacks, few Jews, and even fewer Asians. No Hispanics. Among many other things, ethnic diversity means good and exciting foods from all over the world, one reason to love New York City.

We were defensive of our new way of life but sheepishly confessed that certain culinary matters were lacking. In the city, we had loved going out to eat. It was a pastime all its own, like watching sports. We tried new restaurants and faithfully returned to old favorites. Here, the few choices were less than satisfying and we didn't have the money for eating out anyway.

Just because we had a root cellar full of root crops didn't mean we ate turnips and potatoes all the time. I was determined to make not just a good pizza, but a great one. This upcoming visit from our city friends inspired me. We would take them into the forest for a hike to a wilderness reservoir, go swimming and come home and have pizza.

The day before, I started the sauce. When the stovetop was good and hot, I poured two quarts of crushed tomatoes from the cellar into my skillet. They were red and juicy, just as they were the day I funneled them into the Mason jars. The volume reached almost to the top of the pan, which was a bit risky but with a slow simmer, the level would drop. I put the pan on the hottest part of the stove, nearest the flames. In no time, the tomatoes began to bubble and I pushed it to the back, furthest from the flames, and let it simmer gently. The bubbling subsided. From time to time, I would stir them, adding salt, a few herbs and a pinch of sugar. Some oregano. Lots of garlic. A dollop of olive oil. Within several hours, with only occasional attention, the tomatoes were down to a thick residue in the pan, about a third of what I had put in there.

I decided to top the pie for that night with green peppers and onions and a mix of cheddar cheese and mozzarella. In the morning, I started the dough, a pleasurable exercise. Pizza dough is more elastic than most bread doughs. It is more yeasty and without any sugars or milk, both of which are used in a surprising number of bread recipes. The dough is very similar to baguettes. In fact, I have made pizza dough using a recipe for baguette and it turns out fine. The hard crust is what you are aiming for.

Our friends had spent Friday night in Massachusetts with other friends and planned to arrive at our house after breakfast, ready to hike. I hurried the process. I wanted to have everything ready so that when we got back from the hike, I could produce a pie in short order.

In the early morning hours, I sautéed the onions and the peppers and grated the cheeses. The sauce was ready, cold in its pan from yesterday. As for the dough, I'd learned that if you make dough ahead of time, let it rise and punch it down, you can leave it, covered, in the refrigerator and retrieve it at any time to return to the process. I made up the dough and set it in our root cellar, a.k.a. the refrigerator, for the day.

The day was already heating up. I had our daypack loaded with lunch supplies and towels. Our friends arrived on time. With just a brief exchange of excited hugs and reunion sentiments, we turned right around and drove back out the driveway, on the way to the trailhead for Kilburn Pond. Michael and I often hiked that trail and rarely encountered anyone else in this place, which we regarded as our personal paradise, but in fact it was a huge state park — something like twenty square miles — that had never been developed. As a result, there were no signs or other indications of its existence and the trails were actually old logging roads, as the entire expanse of thousands of acres was really just a big old logging track. The pond was about three miles in on a narrow, winding, wooded path that threaded through stands of ancient, gnarled beech trees and tall oaks. We walked single file, carrying our packs. Moss-banked streams passed over or under the trail. Small animals like chipmunks and squirrels scurried about as we approached. I hoped this experience would convey to our friends what we managed to "do for fun."

By the time we reached the pond, we were sweaty and ready to be refreshed. A beaver slapped his tail and slithered off across the pond. Leaving aside modesty, which was not much in vogue at the time, we stripped down and plunged into the cool green water. Kingfishers scolded. We swam like big fish, around and around until we emerged, climbing back up onto the big boulder

from which we'd launched ourselves. Spreading the towels, we lay
in the noonday sun, the warmth of the rock beneath us radiating
deeply. We talked and ate our sandwiches. Conversation flowed
like the fresh streams all around us. We missed our good friends,
as much as the city pizzas, and wished we all didn't live so far from
each other. It was hard to pack up but there was the hike back.
And the lure of the pie.

Once home, hunger surged. With my rolling pin, I rolled
the dough out on the marble counter, stretching it and stretching it so it would fit onto my cookie sheet. I had begun to push
extra-thin strips of wood into the cookstove to raise the oven temperature up as high as I could. So long as I've had the stove, the
temperature gauge on the oven door has never worked. But I'd
learned to figure out the temperature. I had an oven thermometer
inside the oven and I also knew well how to hold my hand into
the oven to gauge the heat. The rule of thumb was something like,
if the hair on your hand burns off, the oven is hot enough to broil.
My oven rarely got that hot but it did get hot enough to bake a
good pizza pie.

I fit the dough into the pan and spread it with the cold sauce
and then heaped it with the toppings. While I was doing this,
Michael and our friends were out in the garden, picking a salad.
I slid the pie into the oven and whisked together a vinaigrette in
the bottom of the salad bowl, the way my aunt taught me — to
keep the greens fresh. Within an hour, I placed the finished pizza,
fragrant of the onions and the cheeses, hot and tempting, and the
bowl of fresh greens on the table out on the porch. The porch,
open and screened, was warm from the heat of the stove and from

the waning heat of the day but a good breeze was moving cool air in where the warm air had been. We all pulled in around the table and filled our plates.

It was a pizza I was proud to serve to my city friends. They said they'd never tasted one so good. In the city, you wouldn't dare make a pizza — there are too many good ones available at the corner pizza parlor. But up here, finding a way to make good pizza had become a necessity because we wanted it so much. I was glad of that. And, come to think of it, our friends never again asked us what we do for fun up here and eventually, they moved up here too.

Edie's Pizza

1 envelope (1 tablespoon) dry yeast
pinch of sugar
1 cup warm water
1 teaspoon salt
¼ cup johnnycake meal or cornmeal
1 tablespoon olive oil
2½ to 3½ cups unbleached flour

Dissolve the yeast and sugar in the warm water (the sugar helps the rise). After five minutes, stir in the salt, cornmeal and oil. Gradually add the flour, stirring with a wooden spoon as you go until the dough feels pliant in your hands, ready to be worked. Place the dough on the countertop or on a floured board. Knead and keep adding more flour, a bit at a time, until the dough is no longer sticky. When the dough is smooth, form a good ball and brush this with additional olive oil. Place in a bowl, cover with a towel and let it rise in a warm place, 1 or 2 hours, till doubled. Punch down and knead again. Roll out the dough in the shape of your pans. You can make as many as four small pizzas with this recipe or one large one, depending on how thick or thin you like your crust, and also on your oven size. I found this recipe, in a different version, in a newspaper. It was for grilled pizza. When I tried making this on the grill, I felt that the dough puffed up more like flat bread and, as flat bread, it was delicious but I didn't really like it as pizza. So I prefer to bake this in the oven, like any good pizza.

As we all know, pizza toppings can range almost to the absurd but you know what you like best. I like this with onions, peppers and hot sausage, which I sauté in the skillet while the dough is rising.

When I've got the dough in the pan, I let it rise again, about an hour, oiled and covered, because this is a time when the dough can become dry and hard if you aren't careful to cover it completely. Preheat the oven to 375 degrees. Once the dough has risen, I smooth on the pizza sauce, which has to be a thicker variety of spaghetti sauce. I prefer to cook down my own but there are plenty of jarred sauces now that are very good. Put whatever special toppings you choose over the tomato sauce and then cover it all with a mix of cheddar and mozzarella. Add a little Parmesan or romano for extra bite. Place in the oven and bake for about half an hour. Keep your eye on it. The edges of the crust and the cheese should be browned and everything bubbly.

The Common Ground

B Y THE END OF THE 1970S, it seemed that what we made in the kitchen of our little homestead was wholesome and laced with treats. We mastered the art of making hand-cranked ice cream in the summer and we made pizza in the winter. Stews and soups were frequent offerings at our table. Michael was by then a full-time carpenter, hungry at night, and places were often set for the men who worked with him or else neighbors, sometimes even children of neighbors. Whoever came through the door, a place was set and another chair was found. And sometimes, after dinner, we'd play poker. And of course, in our effervescent innocence, there was a good deal of smoking and drinking that went on. It was a good time in our lives. We had provided ourselves a place to live that was warm and comfortable; we lived in a beautiful area of the world and welcomed each season with its particular personality; the panoramic view from our windows gave us perspective as well as full solar advantage, which heated our water and warmed our tile floors; and we loved our neighbors, sparse as they were, the old and the young, and welcomed them to our home whenever possible. I couldn't imagine loving a life in the suburbs where everything seemed constrained and ordinary. I was able to write during the day, imagining and hoping for the day when I might be published. Although our lives were not all about art, it seemed at times as if we were living parallel lives to the artists in Paris in the 1920s or in Greenwich Village in the 1950s. We had fashioned a life that did not cost us much and as a result we were able to live as we pleased. I recall that there was much laughter, music and a strong feeling of togetherness at that time. Quite simply, we loved our simple, uncomplicated lives and were proud of the fact that we did not rely on fossil fuels and power grids. There was a feeling of freedom that surrounded us, which made us happy.

On the rare occasion when we ate out, usually a Friday night, we often ate at a place called The Common Ground in Brattleboro. I loved the name because it was what it really was. The place was known far and wide because the workers there — the cooks and the waitstaff — owned the restaurant in a communal manner. It was a place where revolutionary souls like ourselves gathered and ate and passed information, for instance, about the next antinuclear rally. The food was always good and mostly vegetarian. Everyone who went there could have been your soul mate. Pony-tailed young men in bare feet and worn jeans sat beside their women, whose bare feet emerged from beneath their long skirts. Their hair was as long as their boyfriends'. We all shared this common ground.

A favorite on their menu was Stir-fried Veggies and Tofu. The first time I ever ate this common fare for hippies was in a yurt in the middle of the woods, where a friend of Michael's named Ted had set up a life for himself. Apparently he had had a disastrous love affair and as a result, in my view, he had constructed for himself a life that excluded the need for women. I don't know if this was true but I sensed it, in things he said and the way he cooked, which had a way of saying, "See? I don't need a woman to cook for me. I am perfectly capable of putting a good meal on the table all by myself."

I don't know about variety but he was able to prepare a mean version of stir-fried veggies and tofu over rice. He cooked the rice in a greased skillet on top of his small woodstove, a method that gave it a nutty flavor. He seasoned the veggies with tarragon and served this in bowls, scooping a healthy portion of rice into the bowl first, then the veggies and tofu out of the other skillet and finally, without asking if we wanted this or not, he topped it all with a large amount of plain yogurt. I remember watching him do this the first time and wanting to cry out, No thanks! But he was authoritative in his mannerisms, enough to make me sit by and watch. And then dig in. To my everlasting surprise, I liked it. He served this to us whenever we went there for dinner, a visit that included a long trek through the woods to his unorthodox dwelling — which had no electricity but was lit by Aladdin lamps, a kind of oil lamp with a sophisticated wick that shed more light than the old-fashioned, single-wick lamps. He had gotten them through a mail-order catalog that specialized in items for the counterculture. In fact, we were so impressed by Ted's lamps that we ordered some for our house to replace our old-fashioned lamps. And so, from Ted, we learned about Aladdins and the delight of yogurt on top of our veggies and tofu.

The Common Ground sometimes stepped away from those traditional favorites and one of them was Mushrooms Provençale. The restaurant put out a newsletter each month and in the newsletter, they printed the "recipe of the month." I collected just about any recipe I could find and was eager to adapt it to my cookstove. Therefore, I was delighted when they printed the directions for Mushrooms Provençale, one of my favorite items on the menu. I couldn't wait to try it out.

Unfortunately, whether by carelessness or by design, the recipe was missing a lot of instructions. I still have the recipe as it was printed, torn from the newsletter, the paper as worn as a dollar bill and covered in stains. Here's how it was printed:

Per serving: 5 oz. Mushrooms, whole or cut into bite-size pieces; 2 Tbsp. garlic butter; ¼ cup white wine; 1 cup duchesse potatoes (mashed potatoes with egg yolk, cream and pinch of white pepper); small pinch of cayenne; a pinch of white pepper.

Saute the mushroom in garlic butter over low heat for about two minutes, add the wine and continue cooking another minute or so. Transfer to a shallow, ovenproof single serving dish, add the chopped scallion and the cayenne, top with the Swiss and then the Parmesan cheese, and ring the dish with duchesse potatoes, either squeezed through a pastry tube or placed on with a tablespoon. Place the dish under a broiler for two minutes or so, until the cheese is melted and the potatoes begin to turn brown.

On first reading, I thought this would be such an easy rec- ipe. But when I tried it the first time, I was brought up short by the embedded ingredients not mentioned in the ingredients list — scallions? How much? What Swiss and Parmesan? And exactly how do you make those duchesse potatoes? That first time, try- ing the recipe, we ended up with mushrooms sautéed in wine over mashed potatoes, which actually wasn't bad but it sure wasn't what I had been aiming for. It strikes me now that it was in keep- ing with the times, a casual, inexact recipe that you could figure out for yourself. Apparently I was going to have to indulge in trial and error. Prior to that, I thought all recipes were to be followed as written, at risk of failure if you didn't.

After that first trial, at which time I realized too late that I did not have the scallions or the proper kind of cheese, I made sure I had all the necessary ingredients, intending to make enough for four people — another challenge. My cast-iron skillet was very well seasoned by then. I remember the fragrance of the garlic as it hopped around in the butter and turned golden. Then the mushrooms. When they looked just right, I poured the wine over them and a sweet, musky fragrance lifted into the room. About that time, Michael and a couple of friends burst through the back door. It was a very cold Friday night and we had all planned to gather around our table for dinner and afterward a game of poker. "Whoa! What is that smell?" they cried. It was as if I was pre- paring a wedding feast for royalty. They all but swooned as they crowded around me at the stove, which was invitingly warm and now aromatic. Everyone was so very hungry.

"My God!" cried Peter, one of our neighbors. "You're using *real* garlic?" His eyes, within his bearded face, grew large.

At that time, I suppose, it was more common to use garlic powder if you wanted a garlic flavor in your cooking. Bulbs of garlic were yet another thing my aunt had unconsciously introduced to me. She always used fresh garlic and I simply followed suit. The recipe at hand had called for "garlic butter." I still don't know if there actually is or was such a thing.

While I made the duchesse potatoes, from a recipe I had finally found in a cookbook at the library, the wine was poured and a joint had been rolled. Everyone seemed to be talking at once and what I remember most was the smell of the garlic and the mushrooms and the laughter, all blended in like a thick, rich stew. Someone put Van Morrison on the stereo. The evening had begun.

Mushrooms Provençale, with all my adaptations, became the dish everyone requested when we gathered. It was, to some degree, the same recipe I'd torn off the end of that newsletter but the way I figured out to make it made more sense, and tasted oh, so just right.

Mushrooms Provençale

2 tablespoons butter

2 cloves garlic, sliced

1 pound fresh mushrooms, sliced thick

¼ cup white wine

2 to 3 fresh scallions, chopped

½ cup Gruyère cheese

¼ cup fresh Parmesan cheese

pinch of cayenne

fresh ground pepper

4 cups duchesse potatoes

Preheat the oven to 400 degrees. Heat the butter in a skillet and drop in the garlic. Let it sizzle for a while before adding the mushrooms. Sauté until the mushrooms are brown around the edges. Add the wine and let the alcohol evaporate but not too much of the liquid. Transfer to a shallow, ovenproof dish. I use one that's circular to give the potatoes the best effect. Add the scallions and the cayenne and top with the two cheeses. Ring the dish with duchesse potatoes — either squeeze through a pastry tube or place them around with a tablespoon. Place in hot oven for 15 minutes, until the cheese is melted and the potatoes begin to turn brown. Serve hot.

To make the duchesse potatoes: to four cups mashed potatoes, add 4 egg yolks (Save the whites and have Orange Marmalade Soufflé for dessert!), 3 tablespoons butter and ¼ cup heavy cream or sour cream. Season with salt and pepper. Whip. Serves 4.

PART THREE

The Eighties

Lobster by the Sea

MOST OF OUR FRIENDS from that time in my life are now divorced, as are Michael and I. In a way, it was all too good to be true and then it was over. I was lucky to have found Paul, my second husband and the love of my life. Unlike Michael and me, Paul was a New Englander, born and bred. Michael and I had actually built our house on the road where all Paul's ancestors had farmed and the road was named after them, the Boltons, a big clan who had spent most of their lives working in the woods or farming or carpentering, which is what Paul's father had done and what Paul did. They were mostly quiet and hardworking and their menus were simple — meat, potatoes and pies.

Paul's favorite, though, was lobster. Just lobster, which barely needs a recipe. No sauces or stocks or mayonnaise, please. No stews or thermidors or bisques or Newburgs or curries. Just lobster. If ever there was a special occasion, a birthday or New Year's

Day or an anniversary, Paul would suggest we might want to have lobster. Once, the evening we decided to get married, Paul came up with the idea that we ought to get ourselves a couple of lobsters to celebrate. It was probably five in the afternoon by that time, and it was in the dead of winter. And this was at a time when not every supermarket had a tank with live lobsters crawling around. In fact, there wasn't anything of the kind back then.

"Where are we going to find a lobster?" I asked.

"Let's go over to the seacoast!" he replied in an uncharacteristic swagger.

"What?" I was taken aback. The seacoast was at least an hour and a half away, depending on where we went. And it was a week night.

"Let's go to Maine and get lobsters!" he said, laughing now. No one could laugh as easily or as happily as Paul.

"Maine?"

"Sure, come on, let's go!"

And so we did, laughing the whole way at the madness of our adventure, but sobering a bit when we found most every place we could think of closed either for the season or for the evening. It was very dark, very cold, very January.

We drove north along Route One, and then south again, searching. At last, our voyage was salvaged when we found a seafood restaurant that was still open and serving. What we had in mind was to buy a couple of live ones and bring them home, steam them up and enjoy them, maybe with a glass of champagne. That plan no longer seemed possible. This restaurant was in Hampton Beach, which, in the summer, is almost untouchable, it's so crowded. Not our style. But on that night, there was something about it that suited us. The street, which in the summer is jammed with cars, motorcycles and pedestrians, was deserted. On one side of the road are blocks of shops and restaurants. Some were boarded up for the winter. On the other side, surf crashed in the darkness.

Hardly anyone was in the restaurant when we walked in out of the bitter wind. It was warm inside the bar. By then it was about 8 o'clock in the evening. The waitress was sitting at the bar, talking with the bartender. They both looked up at us as if someone had walked into their living room unexpectedly.

"Do you have lobster?" Paul asked. His glasses had steamed up almost as soon as he'd walked inside so he looked like a blind man, seeking.

"Why — yes," the waitress said.

We were cold and very hungry. There was a wooden booth beside the window, which was adorned with a bright red Budweiser neon sign. The faint smell of salt and beer and French fries lingered in the air.

We slid into our seats and looked around us. The dimly lit, empty restaurant had the feeling of a stage set, waiting for the first act.

The waitress, who was not young, came over to take our orders.

"Actually, we were looking for live lobsters to take home, but we couldn't find anyone open," I told her.

"You wouldn't have found any, Hun," she said. "There aren't many at this time of year and it's been so cold the past few weeks, no one's been going out. This is probably your best bet."

Paul and I looked at each other and exchanged smiles. We ordered steamed lobsters and baked potatoes and salad and beer and when the tray came, we put on the bibs and set to the lobsters with the same gusto we had felt when we'd started out from home. It wasn't quite what we'd imagined but it was great, and after he'd polished off the tail and the claws, Paul sucked all the meat out of all the little claws and knuckles and tails that he could, which was how he took on a lobster. I usually just let it go at the meat that was (relatively) easy to get. He wasn't going to argue with me about that because that left all the more parts and pieces for him to excavate.

If we had laughed on our way over, we laughed even harder on our arrival home, at 1 o'clock in the morning. We were not night owls and our mission struck us funny, as if we'd really both lost our senses over our love for each other and our love for lobster, which seemed to be running neck and neck.

The night we went looking for lobsters became part of our lore, a story we reminded each other of at various times during our years together, which became a marriage saturated with love but framed by illness. Though that near-lunacy was never repeated, we were, in fact, quite often out, prowling the seacoast, looking for lobsters. Usually I was on assignment for *Yankee* and Paul came along to keep me company. But after the assignment was completed, we had to eat. I can remember any number of places where we broke the backs of many a hot, red lobster, broth streaming out the end while we tried to contain everything we could, to extract as much as we could from each crevice, each shell. We performed this ritual in wooden booths at roadside restaurants, at picnic tables on the beach and, most often, in seaside cabins.

Cutler, Maine, was one of the places we visited most often, both for work and for pleasure. The lobster pound there was underneath a float in the harbor and to get lobster, we would walk out to the end of the long high-stilted dock and ask for a couple of good-sized fellas and the man would climb down the ladder to the float (if the tide was high, it wasn't much of a climb but when the tide was out, he climbed down as far as if he were climbing down from the top of a two-story building). Once on the float, he'd lift a hatch cut into the center and reach in to get us what we were after, right out of the sea. Their color was of sea-polished stone and seaweed. These were the best lobsters ever, and we always went back for more whenever we were nearby Cutler.

We often rented housekeeping cabins along the coast of Maine just so we could go to the local pound, buy a bag of lobsters and cook them up at the cabin. An array of kitchenettes, equipped with Formica tables, diner china and kitchen gadgets from the 1950s, and of course, the requisite lobster pot, spin through my memory when I think of the number of places where we stopped, just to have lobster. And to spend the night.

Steamed Lobster

1 2-pound lobster per person

1 tablespoon sea salt

¼ pound butter

1 fresh lemon

Serving lobsters, eating lobsters, is not for the faint-hearted. My mother hated lobster, claiming they were "so messy." True. That's why, when you order them in a restaurant, they come with bibs. Eat lobsters at the risk of your clothes. Buy fresh, live lobsters. When you pick them up, their tail should curl with enthusiasm. Their color should be dark green, like a beach stone. Buy them as close to the time you will serve them as you can. In the meantime, keep them in the fridge in the bags they came in.

Most books will tell you to boil a big pot of water to prepare for cooking lobster. I prefer to steam them. Put 3 or 4 inches of water into a pot big enough to contain the lobsters you bought. Add a tablespoon of salt to the water and bring to a boil. When the water is boiling rapidly, open the lid and drop the lobsters in. Clamp the lid back on quickly! You want to contain the steam and it's just as well not to watch the process of killing the lobsters.*

---

* There are no two ways about it. If you are going to eat lobster, you have to kill them yourself. It's kind of shocking when you think about it, because, with the exception of the oyster, lobster is likely the only remaining creature that we kill ourselves prior to eating. That in itself is a sobering thought. Much has been written about whether or not they feel the pain or whether we feel their pain, or some of each. If all of this really bothers you, don't eat lobster and definitely don't dwell on their last moments of life there in the pot. You'll never be able to enjoy the lobster.

Steam is hotter than boiling water so the lobsters cook a bit more quickly this way than they do in the cauldron of boiling water. The lobsters also absorb less water. When a lobster is boiled in a big pot of water, it takes in a lot of water, making a messy task even messier once they get onto your plate.

Set the time for ten minutes. Turn heat to simmer. Meanwhile, melt about 2 tablespoons of butter per lobster/person in a saucepan. Just melt it, don't cook it and place the melted butter into little cups. Squeeze a good measure of fresh lemon juice into the butter and stir. Set the cups by each plate. Check the lobsters. If they are bright red all over and the antennae come out easily, they're ready to be served. Use a nutcracker or a specially designed "lobster cracker" to break open the shells. Use a pick, the sort often used to prize nuts out of their shells, or a pickle fork, to extract the meat from the fins and from the knuckles.

Icelandic Rhapsody

WHEN I WAS TWENTY, I went to Iceland for the summer to work on a sheep farm. The year was 1969, the year of Woodstock and the year Neil Armstrong walked on the moon and the year of the Charles Manson murders and the My Lai Massacre — a year of turmoil, to say the least. What prompted me to go to Iceland is probably nothing I can explain very well. Everyone was going somewhere, or so it seemed, and the mystery of somewhere different lured me. Before I entertained the notion, I had barely ever heard of Iceland. I was told it was a beautiful place, that Iceland was really green and Greenland was really ice. (That turned out to be true.) One of the many things that lured me was the idea that I could spend the summer eating lamb with the same frequency that we here ate hamburg or French fries. I loved lamb and we rarely ate it at home. There were many delights in Iceland, but one of the grand disappointments was that no one ate very much lamb. In fact, Imba, the teenage daughter of the farmer with whom I spent most of the summer, explained to me, as well as she could through our significant language barrier, that they export most of the lamb they raise. At almost every meal, we ate fish and potatoes, the fish pulled freshly from the big milky river that ran past the farm and the potatoes dug from the garden beside the house. Rhubarb and potatoes thrived in the Icelandic climate, where August feels like early spring. Rhubarb soup, which was delicious, and head cheese, which was disgusting, accented the meal. There were chickens that pecked in the barnyard but we never ate any chicken, either. The little hens were strictly for eggs, the smallest I have ever seen — in my memory almost like robin's eggs, though my memory has probably reduced them to something smaller than they really were.

But sheep were a big part of what we did on that farm. In late June, on the solstice, we rode up into the mountains of Iceland's volcanic interior on our Icelandic horses and herded the farm's substantial number of sheep back down to the farm, where we corralled them and clipped their long, straggling wool. This was an annual event that equaled any holiday we Americans might have. In fact, in many ways, I'd never seen anything like the vigor with which the entire island took part. All the grown children from our farm came home from the city (where all Icelandic farm children seemed to end up, as is the case throughout the world) to help in the sheepshearing, which continued all through the daylit night and into the day following, for as long as it took to shear every sheep on our farm as well as on our neighbors' farms. For the event, Unnar, the farmer's wife and my mother for the summer, prepared a roast lamb. I was so excited about that, I could hardly keep my focus on the sheepshearing, which I was doing for the first time and with a slow pace, relative to everyone around me. Even ten-year-olds, who were able to flip the sheep back and forth and around and down with one hand, the other hand on the scissors (no automated clippers!), were clipping with lightning speed.

Inside the big barn, which had stalls and partitions for lambs and ewes and rams, I was given a crash course in shearing methodology. The clippers were one piece of steel, curled at the top and the two ends sharpened like scissors. The curl served to create tension in the two blades, which could be held in one hand like pruning shears. The other hand held down the sheep. The trick was to get the sheep on its back and let it relax a bit so you could get the fleece started. A complete, singular and unbroken fleece was the goal. I had watched a few of the old grandpapas work to get myself ready. Start at the neck and work to the rear. The wool of Icelandic sheep is dense, and by the time they are brought in for the annual shearing, it is saturated with the elements of an entire year — on the lam. It hangs lank and straggly, often dragging along the ground, an utterly despondent sight.

I shudder at the memory of my first attempt. I held the trembling animal with my left hand and pushed my shears into the wool with the other — I can still recall the sensation of those sharp blades biting into flesh. I recoiled in horror and almost wept for the injury I'd caused. Blood stained the fleece. Old Daniel was watching me and he smiled, knowingly, and said, as best as I could understand, "This happens, keep going. She will heal." And so I did, working slowly.

All around me, the sound of the shears made a rhythmic frenzy. Sheep were led into the barn one by one and as one of us finished our task, another sheep would be given us to shave. Bare-naked relieved sheep trotted out the back of the barn and back into pasture as fleeces piled up like flapjacks in the middle of the barn floor. (Sometime later, Unnar and Imba and I would sit in their living room and wind all the resultant wool into skeins and Unnar would knit sweaters and sell them to a mysterious American man who came and gave her six dollars for each sweater which he sold, retail, in the states. Needless to say, he made quite a profit.)

I got into the rhythm. Every time I stood up to receive another sheep into my stall, my thoughts turned longingly to the roasted lamb I knew waited inside the little farmhouse. If it does not seem impossible, I would say I could smell the roast from inside the barn. I am sure I couldn't but perhaps could imagine it so vividly, having awakened to the smell — that smell of crackling fat was capable of overcoming the much more intense smells of the lanolin in the wool and the manure and all the myriad odors of that big barn and its occupants.

Once, I went inside for a bathroom break and saw, sitting on the kitchen counter, a huge blue oval platter. I can still see it, shimmering like a mirage ahead of me on a dry and dusty highway. The newly roasted lamb lay in the center, dark crackling fat wrapped around the meat, red juices flowing from beneath. All around the sacrifice, Unnar had arranged rings of pale green slices of cucumbers and bright red wedges of fresh tomatoes. For Icelanders (and during that summer, for me) these garnishes were rare and more exciting than any roast lamb could be. In the south of Iceland was a town that consisted almost entirely of green-houses where all kinds of vegetables grew. I had not been there yet but Imba had told me about this place where even bananas were successfully grown under glass for the produce-starved citizens of this Arctic nation. Even so, the harvest was expensive and so, on our farm, tomatoes were bought only for special occasions — like this one.

I returned reluctantly to the shearing madness back out in the barn. When we broke for a meal (since there is daylight all the time, meals come at odd times but work never stops), we all went inside. We squeezed around the long dining room table where usually just Imba, Daniel, Unnar and I gathered. But the long table and benches had clearly been designed to accommo-date many other helpers. We pushed together on the benches and passed around the platters. After a long summer devoid of both meat and fresh vegetables, I remember that meal as if it had been the first meal after a long fast. Excited conversation, very little of which I understood, flowed around me. There would be many more hours of sheepshearing but only one meal of lamb.

For whatever reason, sheep have followed me through my life. Living in the town of Chesham, I was often host to a flock of sheep kept by the local sheep farmer, David Kennard. Wellscroft Farm is well-known throughout New England, mostly for the sheep trials that David performs at fairs and special farm exhibits — his impeccably trained border collies push the sheep here and there to show the dogs' agility as well as the ways of the sheep, dozens of them moving, tightly knotted as if they were one entity, a way they have of protecting themselves from predators.

I've never been to one of David's sheep trials, but I have often seen him and his dogs herd the sheep down from his farm into my pasture when I lived in Chesham. I was always disappointed if I came home to find the sheep in my field, which meant I had missed their arrival, trotting down the road and through the gate, a vanishing pastoral delight in this automated world. In the pasture, the sound of the bells around their necks, ringing as they grazed, gentled me out of the bad moods and lulled me to sleep at night. I learned to recognize their distinctive faces. Like us, some of them had such pretty faces and beautiful, soulful eyes. Others had faces only a mother could love.

In times of weather extremes, I was called upon to feed these sheep, carrying bales of hay and cans of corn to the fence. As a result, whenever they saw me, even if from far across the pasture, a small stampede would result, which somehow made me think they were excited to see me. But, of course, I was just the conduit of their feed, which is what causes all of our hearts to quicken.

David sells fresh lamb, spring and fall, and for the past ten or more years, I've bought from him a lamb, butchered to my order. It's another one of those conundrums: I hate to eat lambs that I might have fed or personally known in some way. It's surely a difficult feeling to deal with. I've known more than one family who raise sheep and decline to name the critters since it's so hard to explain to the children that they are going to eat Alice that night. But the alternative is to buy lamb that might have been shipped here from as far away as New Zealand, which is pretty darn far, and even if it's shipped here from somewhere closer, I have no idea what the lamb was fed or how it was treated during its life. So if I am going to eat lamb, I prefer to eat lamb that has been born in a Wellscroft stall and grazed on Chesham grass.

David brings me the lamb in a big sack, all the frozen pieces wrapped in butcher's paper, sealed with masking tape and marked with the cut. Loin chops, stew meat, ground lamb and shanks are the bulk of the order. Then there are the two legs, the reason, really, why I buy the lamb to begin with. It's been many years now and even more roast lambs have been enjoyed around many different tables, in many different places, but whenever I sit down to a meal with roast lamb at the center, I still think of that big blue platter bearing the Icelandic leg of lamb and its exciting fringe of fresh cucumbers and hothouse tomatoes.

Roast Lamb

Because of all this lamb business, I've collected a lot of lamb recipes over the years, many for Roast Leg of Lamb. I have recipes that call for complicated glazes of honey and cider and another for grain mustard, ginger and red wine. I suppose the combinations are limitless but the best and easiest recipe I have and the one I use the most often calls strictly for coffee, the stronger the better.

> 1 7-pound leg of lamb, bone in
> dozen or so cloves garlic
> olive oil
> salt and pepper
> 2 cups strong coffee
> 1 cup sour cream or Greek yogurt

2 tablespoons flour

salt and fresh ground pepper

Heat oven to 325 degrees. Wash the lamb under cold running water and pat dry. With the tip of a sharp knife, cut small slits in the skin randomly across the top and push a clove of garlic into each slit. Rub the lamb with the oil and salt and pepper and place on a rack in a large roasting pan. Pour the coffee into the bottom of the pan and roast for 2 to 3 hours. Baste frequently. Use a meat thermometer to make sure it's done — 135 degrees for rare, 150 degrees for medium well. Remove from the oven and let it rest for 10 or 15 minutes — allowing the juices to release — and then place the roast onto a platter. For pan gravy, put the pan over low heat until the juices start to bubble. Add the sour cream to the pan along with the flour and salt and pepper to taste. Add boiling water if it's too dry. Whisk smartly until you have a smooth gravy.

Rhubarb Soup

I never really knew how Unnar made her soup. It tasted pretty much like stewed rhubarb only it was thicker. And there was something else I couldn't identify. This is the recipe I've devised that tastes the most like the soup I was served every day on the farm, sometimes at more than one meal.

1 tablespoon cornstarch

½ cup sugar

1 cup water

2 cups rhubarb

2 teaspoons lemon juice

2 mint leaves

Combine the first three ingredients and heat to boiling, stirring to make sure all the cornstarch is dissolved. Add the rhubarb and the lemon juice and simmer for 15 to 20 minutes. Unnar served the soup warm but serve it hot or cold, as you wish, garnished with minced mint leaves. Serves 4.

Saturday Beans

O N Saturday nights, Paul and I often worked at the Bean Supper in Chesham. People came to this supper from a fair distance because the beans had a great reputation. For decades, the beans were made by our pastor, Mary Upton, who eventually retired from the pulpit but not from making the beans. She baked them all day Saturday, in time for the supper at five. Paul and I worked in the kitchen, ladling out beans and cole slaw into the serving dishes and then running them out to the anxious people who sat at long tables, so expectant of their meals, they practically held fork in one hand and knife in the other, bouncing them in their fists on the two sides of their place settings. People began lining up for a seat an hour and a half in advance. And sometimes, it was very cold, standing out there waiting for the beans.

Mary Upton's beans were succulent and sweet, so sweet they were almost like dessert. In fine Yankee tradition, she would never give out her recipe, which I am sure contained molasses and, I suspect, a measure of white sugar as well. And plenty of pork fat. She cooked them in a big electric bean cooker that probably held 30 quarts. It was white on the outside and enamel lined in black on the inside and sometime late in the afternoon, she and her husband would cart this creation over to the school, where the suppers were held. About the same time, various ladies of the church would come in the back door with their fresh baked pies and set them on the long dessert tables. These pies also added to the draw — chocolate cream being the favorite.

Even in winter, the kitchen became hot as we worked in the fragrance of the beans and the meatballs, the other staple of the meal, broiling in the oven. There were usually about six or seven of us who volunteered to work, and we all had our particular jobs, setting the tables, cutting up the pies, making the cole slaw, checking the meatballs and of course, watching over the beloved beans. Often Paul and I grated up cabbages and carrots for the cole slaw and, in a bowl big enough for a horse to feed from, we'd mix in the dressing.

As the hour drew near for the supper, the pace in the kitchen resembled something like the New York Stock Exchange near closing time. The air was fragrant with fresh coffee and molasses. It wasn't long before cars started creeping into the parking lot and the line outside the door would form. There were two sittings and everyone wanted to get into the first sitting, as they knew well that the second sitting sometimes ran out of beans or meatballs. Occasionally, grown-ups and even the elderly indulged in behavior that more resembled children, such as moving up the line supposedly to chat with a friend but in effect, cutting in. I never saw a fight break out but there were sometimes sharp words, all in the pursuit of Mary Upton's beans.

The supper was a fund-raiser for the church, which needed every cent it could manage to attract. Tickets were sold — five dollars each — and counted out for the first sitting. People tried not to push as they claimed their seats, trying to figure out which table would be served first. In the kitchen, Paul and Maggie and I would glance up from our tasks and Maggie might say something like, "You'd think they haven't eaten in years!" Maggie was a little firecracker of an octogenarian who always watched out for Paul and me, as if we were her children. She loved Paul and always had advice for me. "The way to a man's heart is through his stomach," she'd say. "Be sure you always cook good things for that man, because he's a good one."

For herself, she made sure she cut a piece of the best pie and set it aside in one of the overhead cabinets for later. After everyone was gone and we'd done the cleanup, our reward was sitting down (a reward in itself) at one of the tables and serving ourselves the leftovers. This was also risky since by then the beans were usually all gone and the pies, too. So Maggie at least wanted to get her pie. Whenever she went out and cut herself a fat slab from the new pie, Paul and I had a good chuckle between us. Though she never asked me, she always asked Paul if he wanted her to cut him a slice, too — she'd kind of shout-whisper it to him — but he'd always whisper back that he'd take his chances.

So, for many years, those bean suppers were our Saturday beans. We looked forward to them as much as the rest of those folks who stood in line, and if there was a storm, and attendance was down, we'd get to take some of the beans home in plastic containers. Paul sometimes ate them for breakfast and even, lumberjack style, put a pile of beans between two slabs of bread: bean sandwich for lunch.

I can't remember the first time I made baked beans, but I know that I made beans for both of my wedding receptions — which were simple, informal affairs. My first marriage, to Michael, took place in the meadow beneath the old farmhouse where we were living. I carried a large bouquet of Queen Anne's lace that my father picked from the field that morning and I wore a dress I made myself. Sewing has never been my strength and probably my sister was the only one there who knew that I had not quite finished in time, so there were still a few pins in the dress on that wedding day. I think now it was somehow emblematic of the marriage that as a result I walked carefully and, even so, felt an occasional prick throughout that day.

After the ceremony, we laid out a small feast on the long cedar picnic table outside the kitchen door. Of the ham and the turkey, the salads and the rest of all that I made for that day, I was proudest of the beans. Some ten years later, Paul and I were married in the church of the famed bean suppers and had our reception in the old schoolhouse. Good friends helped me provide a bigger feast, for a bigger crowd, and there again, the crown jewel, or so it seemed to me, was that big pot of beans. Its eminence, having simmered all night and halfway through the day in my oven, and then carefully transported to the schoolhouse in the backseat of the Honda, sat proudly on the table, squat and hot and oh so sweet.

Mary Upton's famous beans were made with kidney beans, but I've found that people are passionate about beans and you can spark quite a discussion about what kind of beans to use when making baked beans. I'm a fan and defender of navy beans, also known as pea beans. But some people use yellow eyes or black eyes, black turtle beans or Great Northern, or good heavens, lima beans. There are even recipes that call for soybeans. And all stand ready to defend their preference.

And then there's the bean pot. I've got a collection now of some thirty-seven different styles — they vary more than you might think. My favorite is still the first bean pot I ever had, which belonged to my grandmother, who, to my knowledge, never baked a bean in her life and certainly my mother never did. She kept the pot on the kitchen counter and put loose change in it. It is unglazed on the outside, giving the feel, if not the exact color, of a flowerpot, but the inside is glazed, a glossy deep cinnamon color. The lid is also glazed in that delicious color, with a small hole for escaping steam. (At least half the bean pots I see for sale at flea markets and yard sales are missing their lids, the casualty of time and of the mobility of the human race.)

This ancestral pot has no chips to show for its long journey and in my opinion makes the best baked beans for reasons I can't fathom. If there were a science to which particular style of bean pot makes the best beans, it would be inexact, to say the least. Those beans I made for my weddings are a good example. For each wedding, I made several pots, necessarily in my various style pots. Each pot came out different. Same recipe. Same oven. Different pot. The beans made in my grandmother's beanpot were always the best. Mary's beans were baked not in a pot but in an electric-fired enameled vat. And people who make bean-hole beans (beans "baked" in a fire-heated hole, usually underneath Maine soil) use cast-iron bean pots. Nevertheless, I've tried all the pots, some old, some new, and they all turn out beans that taste different. And so, in my experience, the pot is as important as the recipe.

In addition to bean pots, I've collected recipes over the years and tried a lot of different ones. Almost every recipe I have calls for molasses and I used to use it, all the time. I know that the first pot of wedding beans I made were molasses beans. But some years ago I worked with a woman in Vermont who gave me her bean recipe. No surprise, hers called for maple syrup instead of molasses or brown sugar. This is the recipe I've used ever since — with many additions such as ginger and vinegar.

Along the way, I taught myself to make brown bread, steaming it up in a greased coffee can on top of the cookstove. Though my mother never baked a bean, she did serve beans, B&M, and she bought brown bread sold at the A&P. That was our Saturday-night supper — along with frankfurters (my mother's term for hot dogs) and coleslaw from the local deli. I came to think of beans as incomplete without the brown bread. The traditional New England Saturday-night supper was baked beans, brown bread, piccalilli, mustard pickles, coleslaw and pie.

The Bean Suppers at the church are no more. Mary, in her nineties, is still willing to make the beans but there aren't enough people willing to work the suppers anymore. This is a sad state of affairs. Haydn S. Pearson, a man who lived in this area during the 1930s and 1940s and who authored several spirited cookbooks, wrote, in 1946: "Saturday night is the time for baked beans for supper and the sooner folks who have gotten away from the habit get back to this dish, the sooner the national debt and women's hats will get under control."

I don't know about women's hats but he is probably right on target about the debt. Saturday beans and the suppers they engendered would be a good tonic for a lot of what ails us.

More often now, rather than on Saturday, I bake beans on a storm day. I have come to love being snowed in, no way out until the storm ends. Especially on these days, I get a hankering for baked beans. When a good storm heads this way, I put two pounds of navy beans into the bean pot, cover them with water and leave them to soak in the pot overnight. All night, while the storm pounds the house, the beans plump up. In the morning, the road not yet plowed, I parboil the beans, a gentle process to soften the beans. I'm still in my nightgown and the snow outside continues to race past the window. After a while, I spoon up a few beans, blow on them and if the skins crack open, I turn off the heat and get ready for the bake. The oven in the wood cookstove is already at a good low heat — never above 250 degrees. I drain and rinse the beans. Into the bottom of the pot, I put a small onion, cut in half. The onion adds the same kind of sweetness as the salt pork, without the fat. On top of the onion, I pour the drained beans.

By January, my year's supply of maple syrup is about down to the bottom, ready to be emptied into the bean pot. So, with pleasure, I measure 1 cup of maple syrup into a pint of boiling water and then I add ¼ cup of apple cider vinegar, 2 teaspoons of dry mustard, a teaspoon of ginger, a teaspoon of salt and some fresh ground pepper. After whisking all these together, I pour the mixture over the beans, which usually covers them. If not, I add some more hot water, set the lid on, and into the warm oven they go.

And I sink down into the release of a day all my own. I have a pile of books I save for these stormy days. I choose one and settle next to the stove. The kitchen fills with the sweet scent of the oven beans. The day goes by this way, the luxury of time like the pleasure of a good dessert. The smell of the beans takes me back to the time of bean suppers, Maggie squirreling her pie into the cupboard, Paul hustling hot dishes of beans out to hungry patrons. The memories calm me. Occasionally, I lift the lid to make sure the beans are not getting dry. If they are, I add hot water and tuck them back in for a while. After about six hours, the beans have turned a golden brown. I ladle a few out of the pot and let them cool before I taste. Sweet surrender. I want to eat the whole pot. I start the brown bread steaming on top of the stove. Usually by then the snow has stopped and the road is plowed, leaving silence and the brilliance of the new snow. Supper's ready and there'll be beans for the rest of the busy week.

Vermont Baked Beans

2 pounds navy or pea beans

1 small onion

1 cup maple syrup

¼ cup cider vinegar

2 teaspoons dry mustard

1 teaspoon ginger

1 teaspoon salt

fresh ground pepper

Using a good ceramic two-quart bean pot with lid, soak the beans overnight till they double. In the morning, drain and rinse and then, in separate pan, parboil until the skins crack when you blow on them. Drain. Cut the onion in half and place in the bottom of the bean pot. Pour the cooked beans into the bean pot. Mix together the maple syrup, vinegar and dry spices and add 1 cup of boiling water. Pour this mixture over the beans. Add enough boiling water to cover the beans. Cover the pot and bake in a slow oven (250 degrees) for 6 to 8 hours. Keep an eye on them and add more boiling water if the beans look dry.

Boston Brown Bread

You can't have baked beans without brown bread. I use washed-out coffee cans for baking tins and steam the loaves in the lobster pot.

1 cup yellow cornmeal

1 cup white flour

1 cup whole wheat flour

2 teaspoons baking soda

1 teaspoon salt

2 cups sour milk, buttermilk, or kefir

¾ cup molasses

1 cup raisins

Combine the dry ingredients and in a separate bowl, combine the liquids. Add the raisins to the dry ingredients and then the combined liquids and mix well. Pour the batter into two clean, well-greased coffee cans, filling them ⅔ full. Cover the cans with tin foil or waxed paper and tie with string. Place the cans in two or three inches of boiling water in a large pot. Cover the pot and keep on a slow boil for 3½ hours.

Cod Cheeks and Ale

Paul often came with me on *Yankee* assignments that took me long distances. It always worked out. He didn't care to stay at home while I was away and I didn't much like traveling without him. It was usually car travel, somewhere in one of the six New England states. I was always sent to nice places. A room for one cost the same as a room for two so if we could find someone to take care of our dogs, it was so much better if Paul could find the time to come with me.

In the middle eighties, *Yankee* made an attempt to add the Canadian maritime provinces to our franchise; that is, they wanted to expand into Canada, border-hop as the advertising department called it, and they asked me to go up into Nova Scotia and Newfoundland and find some good places to stay and to eat, places that would tempt our readers northward in the summertime.

Paul and I went up into Nova Scotia several times and were never disappointed. The lodgings available were simpler and less lavish than what we would usually find on the roadways of the "lower six" but we were charmed by them, as if time had stood still. The little motels and guest cottages, many of them painted white with red or dark green trim, dotted the maritimes. Inside, the sheets were white and starchy, the lamps a little dim and the views out the curtained windows often of the open ocean. Beaches were red and sometimes deserted. Harbors were full of working boats and absent of ostentatious yachts.

We liked Nova Scotia.

Our first trip to Newfoundland, we had expected something similar, perhaps more rustic. The ferry, a retired ice breaker that was streaked with rust, took us from North Sydney, at the northernmost tip of Nova Scotia, to Port aux Basques, a nine-hour bronco ride across the North Atlantic. When brawny sailors fastened our car to the lower deck with enormous chains, we had our first clue as to what we were in for. Paul enjoyed the ride, watching in awe as the boat leapt from one mountainous sea to the next, but the voyage left me green, slightly terrified and more than anxious to set foot on solid ground.

Once our car had been unshackled and we drove down the ramp onto the narrow streets of Port aux Basques, we began our rainbow-studded adventure. Newfoundland's natural beauty was abundant. We stopped almost as soon as we set forth to climb a chalky cliff high above the ocean where we were told we would see whales, which we did, as they surfaced, spouted and then plunged back out of sight.

Long roads traveled across terrain that reminded us of the American west, with orange mesas surrounded by flat sands. At times, the beauty was overwhelming. Soon, though, we began to notice a lack of services. Gas stations were infrequent and we passed only one place that called itself a motel — it was a double-wide trailer sectioned into overnight rooms. Cement blocks served as steps up to the doors. We didn't really want to try that one out. But there wasn't much else. And there weren't many restaurants. At all. So we just kept driving. Occasionally, we passed small, dark taverns but they looked unwelcoming to strangers.

Of course, we always traveled with lots of picnic supplies. Our basket had started out with wedges of cheddar, dark bread, raw veggies, chocolate bars, sodas and beer, but after the long sea journey, we needed to replenish. And we were tired. We drove and drove. The evening shadows lengthened. I found on the map a small seaside village and thought we ought to try to find this little town. It had been many hours since our landing and we were starving.

Newfoundland reminded me in some ways of Iceland, especially in its "highways" — there weren't many and so it was hard to get lost. This little town was off the main road, a series of winding roads led to safe harbor. The village was an anachronism. The center of town seemed like a set for a Western movie, with frontier-style storefronts and, it seems to me, board sidewalks. It has been some years now but that is the impression I'm left with. We poked around, looking for a diner or some kind of restaurant, or even a food store. It was late, probably seven or eight o'clock at night, by the time we arrived. Of a sudden, our eyes rested on a big old Victorian house, surrounded by an iron fence. The house itself was worth noticing because it rose above the more modest dwellings all around it. Nonetheless, it wasn't so much the house as the sign out front that captured us. THE VILLAGE INN, spelled out in bold letters. LODGING. MEALS SERVED.

We parked in front of the house and walked with quick steps to the door. I knocked. The door opened just a crack and a young man peered out at us with one eye, the other eye hidden.

"Can I help you?" he said, somewhat tentatively.

"Yes," I said. "Do you have a room for us?"

"OH!" He opened the door fully, looking relieved and a bit sheepish. "Yes, a room, of course!" I think we were the first customers he'd had in weeks, maybe months.

We stepped inside and introduced ourselves, telling him briefly of our long trip. A television set was on in the living room and we could see, in the kitchen down the hallway, a smaller version of our cookstove at home. In the light of the overhead the gray enamel glinted with promise.

"Your sign says you serve meals?" I felt suddenly I had to remind him of that.

"Oh, yes, that we do," he said. Eventually, we discovered that he and his wife — they hardly looked old enough to be married — had come to Newfoundland from Australia, which explained his uneven accent.

"That is great. We are famished," I said.

He took our bags upstairs to our room, which had a wrought-iron bedstead, a patchwork quilt and a window that looked out on the henhouse. He showed us the bathroom down the hall and said, "When you're ready, come down and we'll fix you some dinner."

I can't think of any words that could have been more welcome. I had long since recovered from the stomach-stopping seasickness I had experienced earlier in the day. And to think we would have a home-cooked meal. Paul smiled at me and rubbed his stomach and licked his lips in the way that he often did when he came in from the woods, eager to eat. A man who had traveled almost none at all when we first met, Paul found these adventures very agreeable. In fact, he loved them.

We washed and changed and came downstairs where we were greeted by our host, whose name I've now forgotten, but whose face I have not: cherubic in a dark kind of way, he seemed nervous, as if he had not done this very often. "We have your table ready," he said and showed us into their small dining room. They had set a table for two beside the window, from which we could see the backside of main street.

He poured water into our glasses and then brought us a basket of bread. "We have cod cheeks and halibut tonight, and fried potatoes," he said in the way of a menu.

"What are cod cheeks?" I asked. I wasn't sure I'd heard him right. I thought maybe he was saying a French word I didn't know.

"Well, they are — cheeks, from the cod," and he took his forefinger and thumb and gripped his own cheek and shook it a little to demonstrate that cod cheeks are no different from our own cheeks.

"Oh," I said, and Paul and I exchanged glances. It didn't seem as if this was a choice. "OK! We will have the cod cheeks," I said, maybe a little overenthusiastically, but I wanted him to know we were ready for anything.

"What have you got to drink?" Paul asked.

"We have ale, pale ale," was the answer.

We both ordered an ale.

And so, orders taken, our host retreated to the kitchen and we dove into the bread basket which was nothing more than sliced white bread. I was just reaching my knife into the tub of margarine he had brought out when, to my surprise, I looked out to see our host and his wife walking out the back door and getting into their small car.

"What? Where are they going??" I cried. By then it was well past eight.

Paul swiveled in his chair to see them drive away. He looked at me in complete confusion. "I have no idea!" The house was suddenly very quiet.

At least we had the bread. And the water. We sat there for a good half hour before the little car turned into their driveway again. Once parked, our host and his wife emerged from their vehicle and from the backseat, they pulled out grocery bags.

"Oh, my gosh, Paul," I said. "They went out to the grocery store!" We were both dumbfounded and started to giggle. It didn't even seem real. We had long since devoured the bread.

There was a lot of noise then, coming from the kitchen, the clang of pots and beating sounds and then the aroma of onions. More time passed and the sky outside grew dark. Soon the young man came in bearing two large platters. A small halibut steak, nicely browned, sat next to a pile of what looked like scallops — the cheeks. And then the potatoes, crisp and golden, and as many green beans as could fit on the plate. "And a glass of ale for each of you?"

Yes, we had the cheeks and the ale and scraped our plates. The cod cheeks tasted much like scallops, something my uncle Jamie loved. Whenever scallops were on offer, he turned chef and fussed over the skillet, tending them with his spatula in an almost tender way. He knew that cooking them too long made them rubbery. Bent over the pan, Uncle Jamie never left their side until they were ready to go on the plate.

I know now that cod cheeks are considered a delicacy in places like San Francisco. On the East Coast, the cod are all but gone, the bottom of the sea scraped clean by huge trawlers looking for whatever fish they can scoop up in their enormous nets. In so doing, they've destroyed the cod's habitat. And so cod, along with their cheeks, are mostly brought in from elsewhere. But likely not in Newfoundland, where I'm sure what we were served that night was akin to pig's knuckles or chicken backs — the last little bit of the fish that might be eaten. Nonetheless, that was a meal not to be forgotten.

After dinner, we went upstairs to our little room under the eaves. The wind, which is as common there as the rainbows, wrapped around the house and howled all night long. In the morning, we looked out the window to see our host emerging from the chicken house with a bucket of eggs. A while later, she treated us to another simple, wonderful meal prepared on that little enameled cookstove. And we went on our way.

I returned to *Yankee* with the news that Newfoundland, alas, was not quite ready for the tourist trade. That was then. I've never returned, though I long to. I hear the ferries are much nicer now. And I'll bet there are more places to stay. But I know it's still wild, beautiful country, which, to me, always, has been a balm and a healing source.

Classic Scallops

(or cod cheeks, if you can find them)

There are two kinds of scallops — bay scallops, which are small as your pinky fingernail, and sea scallops which are big as silver dollars and thick as steak. Sea scallops can sometimes be faked, as unscrupulous fish dealers cut shark meat with cookie cutters to resemble the scallop. If all the scallops are exactly the same size, be on alert that these might not be the real thing. Choose scallops that have a bit of a blush, a pink or beige color. White scallops are probably not fresh. Eat them as soon as you buy them. With scallops, every minute counts.

one tablespoon butter
two large cloves of garlic, sliced
14 to 16 sea scallops
salt and pepper to taste
lemon wedge

Melt the butter in an iron skillet over high heat. Place the garlic in the pan and let it brown. Don't let the butter burn but keep the heat high enough so the scallops sizzle when you put them in. Two minutes on each side is enough to yield tender, sweet scallops. Spritz with the lemon after you put them on the plate. Serves 2.

The Great God of Whatever

O NCE, QUITE A NUMBER of years ago, my cousin and his wife, who lived for many years in Katmandu, gave me a jar of chutney for Christmas. They made it themselves, labeling it: Maharaja's Magnificent Mango Chutney. Dark and hot and spicy-sweet, it was every bit as magnificent as the label claimed. It ended too soon. I scraped the jar and licked the spoon. We wanted more.

I had never made chutney before. It had never occurred to me that you *could* make chutney. The only chutney I'd ever known of came in a little jar with a very British label on it, registered to the queen. My cousins were, by then, halfway around the world so asking for the recipe was out of the question. In a cookbook I found a recipe for mango chutney. It had mangoes and pineapple and raisins and lots of those Near East spices like cayenne and cardamom. It was October. I thought I would make a kettle of it and seal it in jars, providing a good supply for us and some extras to give away at Christmas. I imagined I would impress my friends with this exotic treat.

I went to the store for mangoes. There were no mangoes. I went to other stores. No mangoes. No, the produce managers all explained to me, mangoes are not in season now. It would be some months before we have mangoes.

I panicked. How could I make that marvelous concoction without mangoes? I went home to brood.

In frustration, I turned to other cookbooks. I found peach chutney. Pear chutney. Date-lemon chutney. Banana chutney. Blueberry chutney. *Green tomato* chutney. Epiphany: apparently I didn't need mangoes to make chutney. The recipes all had the vinegar and brown sugar in common and many of the spices were the same but the fruits, it seemed, could be just about anything.

I scoured the kitchen. I had oranges and lemons. I had raisins. I had a half-gone box of dates left from long ago. I had onions. And garlic. And I had apples. Plenty of apples. I set the kettle on the stove, turned up the heat and mixed up the vinegar and sugar and spices. It merged into a dark liquor and my kitchen began to fill with a tangy, bittersweet aroma. The syrup simmered and the windows steamed over while I cut and cut and cut the fruits and rinds, sliding them into the pot as I went.

I let it bubble slowly until it thickened, almost like jam, and turned off the heat. When it cooled, I tasted it. Fit for the queen. I wanted to show it off. I had a good big kettle of it. I funneled the hot treat into sterilized jars and capped them. I saved some for us, and the rest I gave to friends. It was my first effort but certainly not my last. Now I make it every year for Christmas gifts.

In a recent conversation about church denominations, a friend remarked that Unitarians worship "the great god of whatever." I don't know anything about that but it struck me as being like chutney. It is a benevolent god that watches over the ways of chutney. Many ways can lead to the same consistent result: wonderful.

Now when I make chutney, I scour the kitchen for new items. I've used green tomatoes and green peppers. Lemons and oranges. I've used pomegranates and added various kinds of nuts. One year, I found a bag of cranberries in the freezer and added them, whole. They stayed round and red and added color and a new tartness. At first, I favored Pear Chutney and Apple Chutney but in recent years, Cranberry Chutney has become my favorite.

Ironically, I have never used mangoes in my chutney. I simply forgot about them as I had so many other things to use, other things that were found much more easily and grown locally. I never missed them. Nevertheless, a while ago, I asked my cousin, who I see very infrequently, about her recipe for mango chutney.

"What was in it?" I asked.

"Apples and ginger and raisins and garlic and chili peppers," she answered, offhand.

"And mangoes," I prompted. "Don't forget the mangoes!"

"No," she said, "no, that was *mock* mango chutney. There were no mangoes in it, no mangoes at all."

Cranberry (or whatever) Chutney

This makes a big batch, so you can make some for yourself and give some away. Use my method and add whatever you might have on hand: pears, apples, pomegranates, even mangoes if you have them. The basic syrup will be elastic enough to accommodate more fruits to a certain extent. Use your judgment but feel free about it. And be creative. Chutney recipes are very forgiving!

↘ Cranberry Nut Chutney

4 cups water

4 cups sugar

3 bags (9 cups) fresh cranberries

6 tablespoons cider vinegar

2 onions, chopped

2 cups raisins

1½ cups walnuts, chopped, or pine nuts

3 tablespoons brown sugar

¼ cup fresh gingerroot, chopped

3 cloves garlic, chopped

the rind of one lemon, chopped into small pieces

Place water and sugar into a large pot and put on medium heat. Stir until the sugar is dissolved and bring to a boil — no stirring. Add all the rest of the ingredients, including any you might dream up on your own. Simmer, stirring occasionally, until it's fairly thick — about half an hour. Allow the mixture to cool. If you are going to give as gifts, sterilize some pretty jars and seal and cap. Otherwise, place it in a hot sterilized jar and store in the refrigerator. It will keep a very long time. Makes 8 pints.

Cousin Mac and Marcia's recipe for

Maharaja's Magnificent Mock Mango Chutney

10 cups (4 pounds) brown sugar

4 cups cider vinegar

4 pounds apples, peeled and sliced

½ cup crystallized ginger, sliced thin

1½ cups raisins

2 tablespoons garlic, minced

1 teaspoon salt

2 tablespoons crushed red pepper

Make a syrup of the sugar and the vinegar. Add all other ingredients. Boil to a "thickish" consistency but don't let the apples get too dark — they will continue to cook as the mixture cools. Pack in sterilized jars. Keeps indefinitely in a cool place. Makes 8 pints.

The Trip to Spring

PAUL AND I HAD what we thought of as our own private holiday, declared when the green stalks of our rhubarb tinted red and when the shad trees bloomed at the edges of the field. We'd wake up on a day when the sun came up strong and pronounce it "our day." We'd take the day off and drive south, down the Connecticut River to where the shad run upstream in the spring.

We started doing this when I was writing a long piece on the Connecticut River, traveling the valley, talking with people who lived beside it or who had worked on the river or who had known it for long years. It was my assignment to experience the river in all its phases. It was then that I learned about shad and the men who come out in the spring, gathering shad in their nets in the middle of the night, lighting their way home with lanterns, their boats heavy with the big fish.

Salmon and shad share the word *anadromous,* which means that they live in the ocean but return to fresh water to spawn. I've read that they fight their way up the river, so determined that some of them, when they get there, are emaciated from the effort. They always return to the same river where they were born, and when they've completed their mission, they die. The men who fish for shad are not usually fishermen the rest of the year but in the spring, they haul their boats and repair their nets and wait for the signs that show them the shad have come back.

Shad are big, fleshy fish, shot through with bones so tricky, it's an art all but lost to know how to bone them. Because I needed to know the river, completely, for my report, I felt I should eat shad, though it didn't appeal to me. Perhaps I had read and heard too much about how much of our toxic environment the river had absorbed to want to eat river fish. Even though I knew what a remarkable recovery the river had made, still, I sometimes passed men and women tempting the river's currents with their fishing poles and wondered if they really ate what they brought in.

In that spring of my research, which is now something like twenty years ago, shad was listed as a specialty on the menu of a riverside restaurant where I'd stopped for dinner.

"What is shad like?" I asked the waiter whose pen was poised to take my order.

He made a small face and said, "It's very *fishy.*"

I ordered the chicken.

But I felt that I had to try shad, somehow. A reporter's duty. So on my way home one evening I stopped at a little red shack beside the road. On its wall was spelled out SPENCER'S SHAD SHACK and, beneath that, in big colorful handpainted letters, *Connecticut River Boned Shad!*

Inside, at a small Formica-topped table, two women sat cutting into the pink flesh of the silver-sided fish in a mysterious pattern, their knives moving swiftly as they talked to each other, the fillets rising in stacks on either side of them. They stopped long enough to tell me that they're open only for a few weeks in the spring, when the shad are running.

"That's what we do in the spring," she said. "Just wait for the shad to come back."

The rest of the year, the little red shack sits empty, she told me.

I asked if it mattered if I got the fish filleted or not.

"Depends on whether or not you want to eat it," she said, deadpan. "The bones in these fish used to be called the work of the devil. Back in the early days of the union."

I asked for a pound of boned shad and she wrapped a hefty slab in cellophane and then in brown paper, securing it with Scotch tape.

(They also had shad roe, something about which my aunt and I had always disagreed. She thought it to be ambrosia. I never warmed to it but then I don't like caviar, either. I bought a package of roe for her as well, froze it when I got home and gave it to her the next time I saw her. I may as well have brought her the Hope diamond.)

The shack was in Haddam, about three hours south of our house and I turned back north then, on that balmy spring afternoon, up along the river valley, the land along the roadsides bursting with the reds and yellows and pinks of spring. I drove along the valley roads, flat and straight, past fields where tractors moved steadily, turning earth the dark rich brown of a farm's promise. I rolled my window down so that I could breathe in the smells of newly turned earth and budding fields wafting on the cool spring air.

In Hatfield, I passed a big white farmhouse with a small sign on the porch. It swung on its hooks. "Asparagus," the red letters announced. I pulled in. In the barn behind the house, a young man was bundling fresh green stalks and cutting the hard white ends off with his sharp knife. He secured the bundles with rubber bands and as he finished each one, he stood them up in trays of water. There were long tables lined with these trays, the asparagus standing soldier-straight in rows — an astonishing quantity. I bought three bundles and he shook out a brown paper bag with one hand and laid them in with the other. The asparagus, I thought as I continued north, might make the shad easier to swallow.

When I got home, where the air still felt like winter and the trees were showing only the tiniest hint of green, I unwrapped the fish and showed it to Paul. "Shad for dinner," I said.

"What's shad?" he asked. Paul had grown up along the Connecticut River but his town was well north of those famous spawning grounds and the fish had only recently returned after an absence of perhaps 100 years.

"It's a river fish," I told him, "and it may not be very good but we can think of it as an experiment."

I had no idea how to fix it. Lying on its mat of brown paper, it looked solid but when I went to pick it up, it fell into long strips. I realized then that that was how the women had taken out the bones: they carved them out and then pressed the fish back together. I decided to dip the strips in egg and then roll them in breadcrumbs, a middling solution. Meanwhile, I prepared to steam the asparagus, my ace in the hole.

I know now that I could have done the fish any old way and it would have been unparalleled. I can still remember the look on Paul's face when he first tasted it — a kind of clouding of the eyes and then a mysterious smile, as if he'd discovered a wonderful secret. He had. We had. It was shad, its flavor and texture unlike any fish, any *thing* we'd ever had — sweet, light, delicate — words fall short to describe it.

That dinner spawned this pilgrimage that took us south every May thereafter, to the shad shack where, each year we bought more and more shad, some to eat fresh on our return home and much more to freeze for future summer meals on the porch.

Paul enjoyed the return to the valley, to his river. Besides, it was so pleasant, the journey south into a season warmer and more open than what we had in New Hampshire, that we made a whole day of it, packing a picnic that we spread somewhere on our way, always at the river's edge, lying back at the end of the meal, feeling the strength of the sun on our winter-white skin. As we drove, we'd point out the blooms in childlike excitement: *Look! Magnolia! Cherry blossoms! Dogwood!!* And when we'd spot the first lilacs in bloom, usually very close to the shad shack, we'd cry out, pull over, and roll down the windows, hoping their intoxicating fragrance would drift our way. At home, our lilacs were still several weeks away from blooming, their leaves then no bigger than a mouse's ear.

We were going for the shad and not incidentally, I suppose, for the asparagus, but what we began to see was that we were going for the spring. A trip to spring, Paul called it. The last couple of years, we got smart and dressed in layers — sweaters over T-shirts, sweatpants over shorts — and when we got to the river and pulled lunch out of the back of the car, we'd strip down and sit in our T-shirts in the warming sun at the river's edge and watch the river traffic.

The ritual grew more elaborate. I rose early on those mornings of the annual outing and baked a pie of the rhubarb that was unfurling in the garden so that we'd have that to add to this spring banquet — shad, asparagus and rhubarb pie. Could there be a headier entrance to summer? I began to see the journey as an obligation to the rest of our neighbors, when we, a committee of two, went south and ushered spring back with us to New Hampshire. Spring otherwise might never have come.

Paul died in May of 1989. A few weeks before he died, we went to get the shad. He didn't want to miss that trip to spring so we went even though he was weak and sick. We drove to Haddam, to the shad shack, and then up to Hatfield for the asparagus. Back home, the rhubarb pie was cooling. We managed the meal but it lacked the promise of other springs. Spring that year seemed indistinct, a blur of time inside the focus of his illness.

But spring comes back every year, regardless of what has befallen us in the months between. Some years passed before I went back to the shad shack. I took two friends and we drove down the familiar roads. It gave me a muted sense of pleasure to watch the season unfold as we cruised slowly south. In Haddam, the red shack was still there, the doors propped open to the warm May air. The woman had the refrigerator behind the counter filled with shad but we bought only enough for that evening's meal. On our way back home, we stopped beside the river, ate sandwiches, and talked about Paul. The river was running high and the wind whipped the surface into waves that lapped up and soaked the banks in front of us. I told my friends what I knew about the shad and about the men who come out at night in May to work the river with their nets in the darkness. It seemed odd to be there, without Paul, but it felt right, that year in particular, to be where, in the spring, fishermen and their wives wait beside the river for the shad to come back.

Shad and Asparagus

Shad has returned to many of the rivers, thanks to the Clean Water Act and to the destruction of many dams that once blocked the passage for returning anadromous fish like salmon and shad. Find fresh shad, which is likely found near big rivers like the Connecticut, the Merrimack and the Delaware. It will be boned, which means the fish will come in thin strips. Roll the strips in cornmeal. In a cast-iron skillet, heat olive oil and put slices of garlic into the hot oil. When the garlic looks crisp, add the fish. It will cook very quickly. At the same time, the asparagus should be steaming. Take the fish out of the pan onto the plate. Top the fish with the seared garlic pieces and serve with asparagus, which

I steam in a large skillet in a shallow amount of water, keeping a medium heat under the pan for 8 to 10 minutes, less if the stalks are very slender. Keep a close eye. You don't want limp, overcooked asparagus, such as might come in a can. You want the stalks to remain a bit crunchy. Aunt Peg and Uncle Jamie would insist on hollandaise sauce, but I like mine with just butter, maybe a squeeze of lemon.

Rhubarb Pie

dough for a nine-inch, two-crust pie
1½ cups sugar
⅓ cup flour
pinch of salt
6 cups rhubarb, cut into ½ inch pieces
2 tablespoons butter

Preheat the oven to 450 degrees.

Roll out half the dough for the bottom crust and place it in your ungreased pie plate — I always use glass plates, which makes the bottom crust crispy. Combine the dry ingredients and mix well. Add the rhubarb and make sure all the pieces are coated. Put this into the dough-lined pie plate and dot with the butter. Cover with the top crust and nicely crimp the edges. With a sharp knife, cut vents into the top so juices and steam can escape. Bake the pie for 15 minutes at the high heat and then reduce the heat to 350 degrees and bake for another 30 to 40 minutes. The top crust should be nicely browned.

PART FOUR

The Nineties &
Beyond

The Summer of Jack

IT WAS MY SECOND SUMMER alone, the summer of 1990, that Jack came to stay. The house needed painting and I had mentioned this to Jack one evening. We were in a writing group together, a group that gathered every Thursday night outside Boston. Jack wrote short stories and seemed to be at a crossroads in his life. After some thought, he offered to come stay with me and paint the house. He asked that in return, I provide him with a room and meals, as well as a very modest hourly rate. This sounded perfect to me. The job needed doing, this fit my budget and I had a spare room. I cautiously looked forward to sharing the house with someone.

The house, a simple Victorian farmhouse, had always been, so far as I knew, white with light gray shutters. In preparing for Jack's arrival, I went shopping for paint. I was about to buy several gallons of white, with smaller amounts of light gray for the shutters, when I suddenly realized it would not cost me anything more to get a color. A new color. It seemed like a radical idea. Instead of buying the paint, I took some paint samples and went home to think about what color I would like the house to be. I had never thought much about house color. I thought about houses that I liked and remembered that several I had seen recently were a lovely deep shade of yellow, with dark green, almost black shutters. As the time for Jack's arrival approached, I accelerated my decision and bought the allotted amount of yellow oil-based house paint, with the darkest green I could find, adding a bit of black to it to make it even darker. I was excited about changing the color of the house.

Having settled on the color, I prepared for Jack's arrival. I made up his room, which was the room Paul and I had used for a bedroom when we first bought the house. It was now a guest room, small with slanted ceilings under the roof and a big closet. That closet was still filled with Paul's clothes. I had given away a lot of his clothing, but I kept things like his red-and-black-checked lumber jacket, his sports jacket, the one he looked so handsome in, and the suit he wore to our wedding. Also in that closet were a couple of dress shirts and a rack of ties. For a man of the earth, Paul had quite a few nice clothes. Also, on the floor of the closet, were his cowboy boots and his wingtip shoes. None of these items ever got much wear but there they were, difficult for me to part with. However, I knew that Jack would need a closet. So I gathered all the clothes in my arms and carried them to the hall closet, and hung them on the rod there, where they stayed for quite a bit longer. The shoes went, too. The closet clean and ready,

I made up the bed and vacuumed the floor. The room looked tidy and ready to welcome a visitor.

I realized, as well, that I was out of practice cooking for someone. I wondered what kinds of things Jack liked to eat. It was summer, a time when the garden was about to yield. By the time Jack arrived, I had jump-started the vegetable garden and was feeling more at home in the soil at this new place. But still, my efforts were thin. Paul had lived in our house only five months before he died and that fact reverberated to me in every corner of every part of the house, every part of each barn, every clot of broken soil. Everywhere I went, there was a hole, a vacancy that could not be filled. The empty side of our bed had become a stack of books and magazines that I was in the midst of reading. The empty chair at the kitchen table bothered me so much that I had finally carried it into the next room so that there was only one chair. The other vacancies were subtler, less glaring, but they were no less painful.

Chief among these were the vacancies in the garden. Cooking for one was a problem but gardening for one, at times, seemed absurd. Paul and I had always planted peas first, sometimes just after the snow had melted and it was always more like a spring event than a task. We had always done this together, as it went faster with two and the specialness of it had become something we looked forward to. As if we were waiting for the first warm day to swim, we watched the weather and waited for the right April day.

When I gardened now, it was more because I enjoyed the activity of being in the soil than the harvest, which had to be rearranged anyway, after he was gone. For instance, Paul loved rutabagas, more than I did. So that first summer back in the garden, I left rutabagas off the seed list. And I planted only a couple of tomato plants. How many tomatoes can one woman eat? Perhaps a tomato a day, for my sandwich? A salad now and then? And I didn't plan to do any canning, which I had always done for the two of us. And a spaghetti dinner was a meal for two, not one.

Jack and I were not lovers. I should say that right away as it was always a question poised on the lips of friends and neighbors. We were friends, maybe even good friends. I could not have imagined being with any man other than Paul at that time in my life, but I did have a deep need for companionship, a need for someone to talk to and, perhaps more viscerally, a need to cook for and care about someone other than myself. I liked Jack. He was a good writer and a thoughtful man. He was younger than I was, by a year or two, and nice looking, with a jet-black goatee that made him look particularly exotic when he wore his beret — usually to literary events, which was often where we saw each other.

Jack had lived in the city most of his life, or what I think of as the city: Boston suburbs. He had a vigorous amount of Sicilian blood in him and he did recall for me the small garden plot his father kept in their backyard. When he arrived early in the spring, the prospect of a garden seemed to tantalize him. He barely had his bags unloaded from the trunk before he stepped into my freshly planted rows, surveying the prospects of future meals. He saw the two meager tomato seedlings and the rows of beans, just up. The potatoes and the green peppers. At last, he saw the spindly shoots of basil and he knelt beside them and gently touched their developing leaves. He looked up at me and asked, "Do you know how to make pesto?"

I had had pesto once in a restaurant and had not particularly liked it. Too much basil, I remember concluding. I wasn't even sure why I planted the basil in the garden. I think I included it to fill some unwritten herb code. Parsley, thyme, rosemary, sage, basil.

"No," I said. "I haven't ever made pesto."

"You should try it," he said. "But you'd need to plant more."

"How much more?"

"Oh, a few rows," he said.

Rows? I have always thought of herbs as — herbs. Subtle, stored in expensive jars, something you sprinkle on lightly to add a teasing flavor. Rows are for real vegetables, beans or peas. I thought about it that night. In the morning, I planted three rows of basil, next to the parsley, which I have always grown in abundance.

They flourished, the thin rows growing into virtual hedges.

Jack and I settled in together, a possibly awkward pair, but it never seemed so to me. I brought the chair back in from the other room and the kitchen table had life again. He went to work, caulking the old windows and glazing the panes, preparing the house for the new coat of paint. It was a wonderful feeling, getting all the work done, yet there was a slight undercurrent of sadness, reminding me of how much I had lost. Jack was considerate and helpful and kind and yet he never intruded on my life. We developed a routine, which assembled itself rather soon after his arrival. He rose at 6 every morning and wrote for two hours in his room before descending the stairs and joining me in the kitchen, where he made coffee for himself, passing boiling water through a plastic cone filter that held ground coffee, letting it drip into his coffee mug, which was considerably smaller than his fist. As he performed this morning ritual, the rich smell filling the room, he told me about his night, how he slept, if he dreamed.

Jack was constantly in motion, picking a dish out of the dishwasher, slicing a bagel in half, wringing the coffee filter out with both hands over the sink before tossing it into the compost, talking all the while. Yet, just as quickly as he came down the stairs, he would disappear outside to the shed, where he gathered his radio and his tools and set up shop near his ladder and began the long day.

By that time, I would be off to work. But I always came home for lunch, the house being only a few miles from *Yankee*. When I pulled into the driveway, he would be working away, most often up on the ladder. He would always wait for me to invite him in for a sandwich, which I would fix for both of us, turkey and lettuce and mayonnaise and mustard, almost the same sandwich every day and almost every day he would say, some halfway through the meal, "Boy, that's a good sandwich."

When the garden began producing, I would add a thick slice of tomato to our sandwiches. I was sorry that I hadn't planted more tomatoes, as it turned out that Jack could eat an abundance of them and loved a few deep-red slices, warm from the garden, on his sandwich.

When the light outside paled, Jack climbed down off the ladder and came inside. He cleaned up in the shed, using squares of my old burgundy sweatshirt soaked in turpentine to rub down his hands and get in around his fingernails.

While he was cleaning up, I fixed dinner. He was not fussy. Spaghetti. Stir-fried vegetables. Whatever I ate was OK with him. In he would come, trailing a faint scent of the day's work, and settling into his chair at the table. This was when he was really ready to talk, an almost nonstop rush of words, as if he'd stored them up all day long. Stories about his father; stories of broken love affairs and disappointments. And then, at the end of the meal, he would rise and politely say, "I guess I'll try to get in a few words before bed." And go upstairs to his room, where he would write for a while, but I never saw the light coming out from under his door after 9:30.

In July, as the basil leaves burst into their finest, greenest, most muscular leaf, Jack mentioned pesto again, in the way a man who loves a sizzling, tender, barbecued steak might mention steak. "Do you know a recipe?" he asked.

I thumbed through some of my cookbooks. Nothing in *Fannie Farmer*. Nothing in *Joy of Cooking*. Nothing in *Good Housekeeping*. Finally, in an offbeat paperback that my sister had given me for Christmas one year, there it was — pesto.

The recipe called for three cups of basil leaves and a cup of fresh parsley. Jack was up on the ladder, scraping the paint from the south side of the house, where the paint had almost completely peeled off the old clapboards. When Jack was at work, he rarely

looked up from his task, as if the work itself was a form of medi-
tation. The day was particularly hot and he was working with a
red bandanna tied around his head, Indian style. I walked past
the ladder on my way to the garden, with my scissors and my
basket. Once I was in the rows, the fragrance of the basil was
overwhelming. I could think of nothing else that yielded such
fragrance except the one rose I grew in the garden and the needles
of the big pine tree beside the driveway. I sheared a good portion
of the first row of basil. Then I scissored a bouquet of parsley. I
was doing this mostly to please Jack. It seemed like an immense
amount of basil to me.

Inside, I pressed the soft green leaves into the measuring cup.
In fact, I had not cut enough and had to go back out, basket and
scissors in hand, for more. When I was done the second cutting,
my fingers and the backs of my hands smelling like the end of
summer, I had less than half my proud green hedge remaining.

In the blender, the basil swirled with the parsley, a deep
green sea. To that, I added several cloves of fresh garlic and olive
oil. Then walnuts — though the recipe called for pine nuts, I had
only walnuts and hoped they would do. Finally, the Parmesan
cheese, which I had grated by hand from a heavy chunk that had
been well aged.

The kitchen filled with the basil's rich scent. Inside the blender's glass, the mixture at first seemed dry and the motor labored
under the work of grinding all those dense leaves. But I kept the
blade moving, pulsing on and off, pushing the leaves down and
down with a mallet. At last, the deep green leaves acquiesced, pro-

ducing a rich paste. The aroma was so intoxicating that breathing it was almost like eating it.

Jack came in from his work, late in the afternoon, the scales of my house paint under his nails and flecked generously on his skin and hair. "What's for dinner?" he asked as he came through the door. He was always cheerful, and in fact, I had been waiting to surprise him with my answer all afternoon.

"Pesto," I said.

I did not need to say it for he had smelled it and seen it in the blender, green as a spring hillside, by the time the word had left my mouth. His face lit up.

"Over noodles?" I asked, tentatively, as I had learned that Jack was very good in the kitchen. Occasionally, when he felt in the mood, he had cooked some wonderful meals for me.

"Sounds great!" he said as he headed for the shower.

I had cooked up a good measure of penne pasta and grilled some hot sausages, which I sliced up and tossed in with the pasta. And then I added in the pesto. This pesto was not anything like the pesto I had once had in that forgotten restaurant. Maybe it was the freshness of the basil or that specific recipe. Even Jack was impressed, downing one, two, three helpings, a fact that pleased me in some deep place I had forgotten I had.

The batch lasted for a couple of days — the last bit of it I used as a topping for pizza, at Jack's suggestion — and there was enough in the hedges for another double recipe. But soon, the hedges were shorn and the leaves had taken on that hint of licorice, the late summer bitterness, a quick end to a long summer of growth. From the last batch, I saved out several containers and put them into the freezer.

Jack finished painting the house in the early fall. He came back to help with a few things but our time together was over. He returned to the city and we stayed in touch by phone and occasional visits. It was an odd, almost mysterious time that we spent together. At the end, I had exhausted the small fund that I had put aside for the work that he did. And he was anxious to get back to his friends in the city.

I do not know what needs Jack had when he came to live with me that summer, but whatever they were, he kept them to himself and gave me the great gift of his friendship, his respect for my probably stifling sadness, and his very capable help around the house. What I had when he left was a beautiful new exterior to the house and a new way of being in the house. Oh — and a love for pesto.

Basil Pesto

(parsley and mint pesto, too)

3 cups fresh basil leaves, stems removed and packed well

2 large cloves garlic

½ cup walnuts or pine nuts

1 cup fresh parsley, stems removed

¾ cup freshly grated Parmesan

½ cup olive oil

2 tablespoons melted butter

Pack everything into the blender and blend on low, pulsing. It takes a while for the density of all the leaves to break down, so be patient. Gradually work it into a smooth paste. Add a bit extra oil if you need to. Serve on hot pasta or as a pizza topping or slather on a fresh slice of French bread. It's rich and potent. An easy variation if you don't have a good crop of basil is **Parsley Pesto.** Make the recipe the same way, only use all parsley. The recipe is surprisingly flexible. Another variation, good with roast lamb, is **Mint Pesto,** using half mint leaves and half parsley, and otherwise following the same recipe. Makes about 5 cups.

Sunday Suppers

A SHORT WHILE AFTER Paul died, I met a woman named Rosemary. We had a friend in common who was dying of cancer. Betty was a neighbor of Paul's and mine. She and Paul had been diagnosed roughly at the same time and they went through treatments together. Betty lived almost another year after Paul died. I baked apple pies for her, as she had told me this was the one thing she craved during radiation. But soon even the apple pie was unappetizing and, as her disease progressed, she began to fade into frequent sleep and hazy recollection. Her friend Rosemary sometimes came to visit at the same time I did and so, sitting on either side of the bed, Betty asleep between us, Rosemary and I began a friendship that has lasted ever since.

Rosemary, so far as I could tell, was alone. I gathered she was divorced and she didn't mention children so I felt a kind of kinship with her as our friendship grew. A tall, elegant woman, Rosemary was in her sixties at the time, old enough to be my mother, but she had a sense of fun and a love of storytelling that made her feel like a contemporary. She had been a nurse, she told me, and I had recently experienced Paul's death and so we shared an interest in the passage from this life into another. She was also grieving the loss of her close friend, Hallie. Both nurses, they had worked together at the hospital and apparently shared a sense of humor. Once, Rosemary told me a story about a dream she had had after Hallie died. In the dream, Rosemary's phone rang and she picked it up to find Hallie on the other end. "Rosemary!" she said. "Can you believe it? We've finally outsmarted Ma Bell. I can call you for free now!"

"I woke up laughing," Rosemary told me.

It turned out that Rosemary had six children and she was married to a man who had left her when the children were still in school, but they had never divorced. So she was alone, and not alone, a kind of limbo that haunted her at that time. She loved her husband and held out hope that he would return. I was in the same place at that time, as Paul's spirit had stayed with me, or perhaps other people might have said I stubbornly clung to it. Whichever, I understood her feeling of suspension. And she understood mine. "Call me anytime, Edie," Rosemary said to me early in our friendship. "You can call me in the middle of the night, if you feel you need to talk."

I wonder still if she knew how generous her offer was, how it comforted me to know that I could, if I needed to, reach someone during those, what had become, darkest hours. It was like having an insurance policy that covered the possibility of panic. I never took her up on her offer but I did call her, often, later in the evening, 9:30 or 10, a time when I felt the need to hear another human voice before sleep. Sometimes I even fell asleep while talking with her. She was not insulted but seemed to understand that the soothing conversations were able to give me what often eluded me: sleep.

Inside Rosemary's elegance lived a big, raw-boned woman who had a way of walking — she liked to point out that she wore a size twelve shoe, in case you hadn't noticed — that was deliberate, as if she were on a mission or making a fast exit offstage. I never quite knew if she was in a hurry to get somewhere or in a hurry to get away. Either way, she hustled, duckfooted, here and there. She always wore long skirts and jackets, the sleeves rolled partway up, and flats. No jewelry or make-up but a colorful hairband kept her steel-gray hair from falling in her face. Her piercing dark-blue eyes were what I noticed first about her. In her eyes shone the wisdom of an old squaw and the insight of a seer. She made me think and she made me laugh. What more could you ask of a friend?

Rosemary did not like to cook — she tried to make dinner for me once, such a disaster we laughed about it for years afterward — but Rosemary loved to eat. "Just something simple," she would always say when I called to invite her. "The point is to be together and share a bit of food."

Rosemary was a Catholic. I almost wrote that she was a devout Catholic but realized I don't know what that means or how she might fit into that commonly used phrase. For periods of time I knew her to go to Mass faithfully and yet it was a private ritual she performed, getting up early and driving to the church by herself, attending Mass and afterward conversing with the priest, which she always enjoyed. She would sometimes tell me stories about Father Tom but they were usually tainted with humor, and I pictured her, at the end of Mass, greeting Father Tom — who, in my mind's eye was middle-aged and somewhat round — holding onto his hand, no longer a handshake but now a gentle form of imprisonment, and telling him a joke, maybe a bit off-color. A lot of these jokes started out with an Irish priest going into a bar. One of her favorites was, "Did you hear that the Pope has bird flu?" She would let a couple of seconds pass and then she'd deliver, in a conspiratorial whisper and with an earnest face: "Yes, he got it from a cardinal."

Whenever Rosemary told a joke, she beamed her eyes directly into yours and, after the punch line, she'd open her mouth to a mostly silent laugh, like a mime on stage, urging you to laugh with her.

She brought this with her to the table: "Whenever two or more of us gather in His name, He is with us," she'd often say as we sat down together. Or perhaps something about breaking bread together. There was always a way that she would insert this tone of religiosity into our get-togethers, in a lighthearted but nevertheless sincere way, she would make our meals seem like a form of communion, the bread and the wine and the gathering of more than one to bring conviction and strength to the ritual of what was otherwise just sustenance.

And so this was Rosemary's own version of Catholicism, a true hunger for a spiritual life but on her own terms. Once, we attended church together and when we rose to go forward to receive Communion, she took hold of my hand, pulled me close and whispered to me hungrily, "I want it *all!*" and then she gave me her mischievous wink and grin before hurrying forward to receive the host.

Rosemary lived simply in the house her husband had designed and built for her and the children in the 1950s. Once he and the children left home, Rosemary occupied it but did not fill it. There was an emptiness about it that she sometimes filled by renting out rooms to make ends meet. Of course, each of these unsuspecting people entered her home, in need of a place to stay for some short period on their lives, thinking they were going to get just a bed to sleep in and the kitchen to share with an older woman, not knowing that they had entered a drama into which they would now be playing a starring role. Those who came to fill one or another of the children's empty bedrooms became a part of Rosemary's tribe, as she watched them and hovered over them, counseled them and guided them on their path. She never stopped being a mother to whoever needed her. Without exception, all of them loved her and remember her as someone who made a difference in their lives.

And so we often had supper together. To make up for the fact that I always did the cooking, she would sometimes take me out for dinner. Friendly's was her favorite. Everyone knew Rosemary. I always felt I was walking with a celebrity. Friends would stop her in the street or swivel around from the next booth to greet her. "Rosemary!" they would exclaim and clearly they felt deeply about this energetic and compassionate woman.

But mostly we ate at my house. Those late-night phone conversations usually ended with a suggestion that we get together for dinner and often it turned out to be Sunday evenings. When we got off the phone, we'd have a plan and I'd look forward to it and plan the menu during the week.

For Sunday supper, I would make something simple, just like she said. A favorite was chicken and dumplings, which was one of Paul's favorites, too. In fact, there was a precedent to my suppers with Rosemary and they went back to my time with Paul. We had a neighbor, also named Paul. (I differentiated them by referring to "Neighbor Paul" and "my Paul.") Neighbor Paul lived in a rundown farmhouse, the next house to ours but actually about a quarter of a mile away. His was a complicated story that involved an old man named Edgar Seaver who had passed away and left his farm to Paul, though members of the old man's family contested that and so at the time that we first knew Paul, the case was hovering in the courts. The farm, with its lakefront land and open fields looking out at Mount Monadnock, was valuable and well worth fighting over. In fact, everyone seemed to want to stake a claim of some sort. Or wrench the whole piece from Paul somehow. With title to that estate, Paul could have been a millionaire many times over. But he chose to live as he wanted to, in the way that he felt most comfortable.

Paul was in his late fifties, I think, and at the time he worked for a defense contractor in Nashua. It was a pretty good job, from what I understood, but the lawsuit over the farm had left him deep in debt so his car was never in good shape and sometimes he had accidents. As a result, he often hitchhiked back and forth to work, a distance of fifty miles one way. This brought him into contact with all kinds of folks. When his car was running, you could see the remains of his meals on the floor and in the back-seat: potato chip bags and Slurpees from 7-Eleven, hot dogs right out of the package and bags of prepopped popcorn. In fact, the car became a kind of capsulized dwelling for Paul, what he some-times referred to as his "mobile home." The heating system in the old farmhouse was nonexistent and so in winter Paul even-tually took to living in his old Dodge Dart, which had a strong heater. On cold nights, in the dooryard of the old farm, Paul would snooze with the car running through the night, Edgar's cat, Tiger, beside him on the seat.

My Paul and Neighbor Paul liked each other quite a lot. My Paul and I both enjoyed hearing Paul tell his stories, stories about Edgar, who was, coincidentally, a distant relative of my Paul's, which added interest, and stories about his legal woes, which left us with the impression that Paul was pretty smart and also stub-born as the day was long. And so whenever I was making chicken and dumplings, my Paul would suggest he go up to Paul's and bring him down for supper. Often, this was on Sunday nights. Paul never turned us down, that I can recall. On invitation, he'd come in through the back door, take off his layers of jackets, tuck his knees under our kitchen table, set his elbows on either side of the plate and gently rub his hands together with pleasant anticipation. He came with the kind of hunger any cook craves. He'd plunge into the dish as soon as I placed it in front of him, the chicken and the vegetables redolent of wine and herbs, and he'd talk while he ate, doing both with equal enthusiasm. About halfway through, he'd usually stop his story and say, "Edythe [he always called me by my full name], how do you get this to taste so good?" At the end, there were just bones in the bowl, so clean they almost appeared to have been polished.

For a man who lived much of the year in his car and who often was left by the roadside in search of a ride, Paul was remarkably resilient, and a man marked by gratitude. I never heard him complain (except in regard to the legal bowl of spaghetti that surrounded Edgar's estate) and often heard him speak glowingly and with gratitude of friends who had helped him, in whatever way, along his unorthodox path. He knew he had chosen his lot and never failed to notice that it could be worse. Once, one night when the temperature dipped below zero, my Paul and I pulled him out of his car, finding him faint and hypothermic. We brought him down to our house and set him beside our woodstove to thaw. An orphan who was adopted as an infant by a family in town some eighty years ago, Paul has no family — except for those of us who have chosen him to be part of our world. He has known some of the worst circumstances imaginable, is the first in line at the rummage sale to purchase this year's wardrobe, buys his cars on swaps and spare change and simultaneously has fought off some of the wealthiest and most powerful men in the region who have approached him in hopes of acquiring his land. Easy to dismiss at a glance, Paul is a speck of holiness in an unholy world.

And so, serving chicken and dumplings for Sunday supper had precedent. I don't actually recall the first time I made it. I can remember my aunt teaching me to make fricassee but never dumplings. I remember vividly my mother once making dumplings. I can't imagine what prompted such an adventure for her but they turned out predictably like heavy weights that would quickly sink to the bottom of any sea where they might be dropped. Making dumplings that would be celebrated seemed like a real challenge. I'd actually never had a dumpling that tasted good, so I'm not sure what inspired me to make them the first time. But even though dumplings can be made to accompany a wide variety of dishes, I only wanted to couple them with chicken, a faithful marriage.

The procedure involves another item that I once spurned: the crockpot. I recall that a distant relative gave a crockpot as a wedding present for my first wedding, to Michael. At that time, we were gradually disavowing all appliances and anything that used electricity. And so the crockpot became something of a puzzle. What to do with the generous gift from the well-meaning relative? I had no intention of using it. But it seemed so callous to give it away or even worse donate it to the rummage sale. And so, feeling some guilt, we set it in the basement in its box.

After those years of taking our vow of electrical chastity had passed us by and Michael and I returned to the workforce and as well to our old habit of eating meat, I remembered the crockpot and I recalled that the best thing about a slow cooker was that you could set something to stew unattended for a number of hours, a good thing for the working world. And so I went down into the basement and recovered the gift, as good as new inside its dusty box.

Under the glass lid of the ceramic-lined urn was a little cookbook for the crockpot. The pamphlet was only about a dozen pages long, but it offered some basic recipes: chili, beef stew and "chicken in the pot." I chose that recipe for the inaugural voyage.

With a few adjustments, I've used that recipe ever since. My addition to it was the dumplings. For that, I turned to what I consider to be the gospel, *The Joy of Cooking*, and found "Dumplings" on page 420. I set the chicken to low and went off to work. When I got home, I opened the *Joy* to the dumpling recipe I'd found the night before. I was very wary, to say the least, because even my aunt Peg was not confident when it came to dumplings. But these were, dare I say it — easy! And that's how I've made this wonderful dish ever since, most especially for Rosemary and for neighbor Paul, who, I came to realize, are two of the best friends I've ever had or could hope for. And so it is with chicken and dumplings, a good friend for Sunday night or any night of the week.

CHICKEN AND DUMPLINGS

Crockpot Chicken (adapted a bit)

You don't have to use a crockpot for this, but it is definitely better when cooked in a slow cooker.

  2 carrots, cut into 3-inch lengths

  2 stalks celery, cut into 3-inch lengths

  2 onions, cut in quarters

  1 whole broiler/fryer chicken, 3 to 4 pounds, cut into pieces

  1 teaspoon herbes de Provence or thyme

  1 teaspoon salt

  fresh ground pepper

  ½ cup white wine (or broth but the wine gives it an amazing flavor)

Put the carrots, celery, and onions into the bottom of the pot. Arrange the chicken pieces evenly over the vegetables. Add the herbs, salt and pepper. Add the liquid. Cover and cook on low for 6 to 8 hours or on high for 3 to 5 hours. Try not to take the lid off very often, if at all. Add more liquid if it seems necessary. Serves 4.

Dumplings

1 cup flour

2 teaspoons baking powder

¼ teaspoon salt

1 egg

milk

fresh parsley, chopped

Whisk together the dry ingredients. Break the egg into a measuring cup and add enough milk to make a half a cup. Beat well and add to the dry ingredients. Add parsley if you choose. The dough should be stiff, almost like biscuit dough but still sticky. On a floured board, divide dough into four equal parts (you can make eight smaller dumplings, if you prefer). Roll each piece between your hands to make four balls. Ladle 2 or 3 cups of broth out of the crockpot into a saucepan and bring to a slow boil. Drop the dough balls into the broth and cover. Simmer for 2 minutes. Turn them over and cook for 2 more minutes. Serve at once with your chicken. Makes 4 large dumplings or 8 small ones.

At Home in the World

I TRAVELED A LOT in those early years after Paul died. I
suppose that is the most natural way to heal, to leave and
seek newness elsewhere. I always had a companion or compan-
ions. Very soon after Paul's death, I traveled to the Caribbean with
Paul's youngest sister, and a year later I flew to Eastern Europe for
a tour with his older sister. On the anniversary of Paul's death,
I went to Scotland with Aunt Peg and Uncle Jamie and, much
later, I sailed with friends off the coast of southern Mexico. To
Provence with Rosemary, to Hawaii with my sister and to Sicily with friends. Like the lamb in Iceland (and, oh, the whale
meat!), I can remember places most vividly by a single meal, even
a taste.

I remember so well, late one night in the waters somewhere south of Puerto Vallarta, the tropically colored mahi-mahi
that our hostess, Susan, hauled in off the side of the boat, a big

beautiful ketch that she and her husband, Brendan, had salvaged and rebuilt in their home port of Australia. They used mahogany and rimu, an exotic wood native to Australia, for the job, rubbed it to an almost unnatural gleam, christened it the Mana Maha, and then set sail to circumnavigate the world. When they reached Mexico, my friend Jane and I flew down to join them and sail farther south, however far we would get in two weeks' time. Nights, sitting in the cockpit in the sweet darkness, we often grilled fish. Brendan had a small charcoal grill clamped to the stern. He used driftwood we'd collected on the beach earlier to start the fire and then fortified that with bricquets. While he readied the coals, we'd play with the phosphorescence, sometimes fill the bucket with seawater and pour it onto the deck. The water flowed across our feet like a miniature constellation. Susan coiled a rope, threw it overboard and pulled it back. Bright sparks clung to the rope transformed into a brilliant, glowing snake. The magic show ended when Susan, a miraculous onboard cook, placed a platter of the grilled mahi-mahi, fresh baked bread and carrots and rice in coconut sauce on the hatch cover and we all set to it.

Then too I remember the incredibly smooth beer that was made in the back room in every tavern we visited in Czechoslovakia and served to us at long tables where we gathered like soldiers in from the war. With the beer came vodka and big plates of sausage and cabbage in an indescribable sauce. I remember the chocolate in Budapest and the marzipan in Sicily, where we walked a long way on cobbled streets and down an alley to find the little shop that sold the sweets, some of them molded in obscene shapes, a surprise and a mystery to me. And also in Sicily, we ate deep-fried calamari off big white oval platters set before us in a beachside restaurant. Through large plate-glass windows, we watched waves break on the white sand and after, we went walking on the beach, picking up shells and smooth stones. I have those beach finds somewhere but it is much easier for me to find the calamari in my mind's eye.

In Wales, in the small town of Laugharne, Aunt Peg and Uncle Jamie and I found a rocky beach and a deserted chapel. Parking our rented red Ford Fiesta beside the stone chapel, which was overgrown with vines, we explored the chapel and then settled on the edge of a squat sea wall, spreading our picnic beside us from supplies that we had stocked up on as we drove. Above us on top of the hill, we had just visited the house where Dylan Thomas once lived and, a few steps farther, his compact writing studio, an old boathouse that a wealthy woman who believed in him had given him to use as a writing place. After his death, the shed, painted robin's egg blue, had been turned into a shrine, a glass front affixed so that we might peer into the interior, turning us into well-meaning, good-hearted voyeurs.

Inside, the bookshelves were in disarray, the red table strewn with poems, crumpled papers lay about on the floor. The sign told us that it had left been just as they had found it when Thomas died, at the age of thirty-nine from what was recorded as "a massive insult to the brain." Otherwise known as acute alcoholism. At the time of his death, he had been in a bar in New York City and finished off eighteen Scotches. Back at his hotel, he had written in his journal, that this was "some kind of record." And then he died.

Down on the beach, we reflected on all of this. It was 1990 and Paul was just one year gone. We realized, with strange irony, that Paul, a sober man, had also died at the age of thirty-nine. And wasn't that how old Christ is reported to have been when he was hoisted to the cross?

"And, oh, what about Sylvia Plath?" Aunt Peg said. "Wasn't she thirty-nine as well?"

"That's weird," I said. "I think that even Grace Metalious died when she was thirty-nine. I just did a story about her life in this little town in New Hampshire. She published *Peyton Place*, her first book, and it became a huge best seller. I don't think she could take all the publicity. I believe she drank herself to death."

And then there was Jack Benny, to whom the age of thirty-nine was like a joke, a number beyond which no one would want to live. Or admit to the fact that they had. On Paul's thirty-ninth birthday, he woke up, stretched his arms toward the ceiling and said, "This is as old as I'll ever be." I never knew if he playing on that old Jack Benny joke or if he was being prophetic. Whatever he meant, it happened to be true.

We talked like this for a while but drew no conclusions.

Fresh strawberries, fresh bread, clotted cream, Stilton blue cheese and Whitbread beer rested between us and around us and we shared these treats as we talked. I remember, especially, the strawberries. It was June and we found them everywhere we went. From the box, Uncle Jamie picked up one of the big, ripe heart-shaped berries and held it by its stem between thumb and fore-finger. He plunged it into the thick cream, raised it as if making a toast, gave me a wink and devoured it.

A few days later, at the Argyle Arms, a hotel and restaurant near Crinan, in Scotland, Aunt Peg studied the dessert menu after a big meal that had included the infamous Scottish "treat," haggis (something like Iceland's dread head cheese) as appetizer and lamb stew as entrée.

"Gad!" she cried out. "Pavlova!"

I had never heard of Pavlova but she convinced us to order it, a soft-centered, light-as-air meringue. The dish, she explained, had been invented in Australia back in the 1930s to honor the visit of Anna Pavlova, the great Russian dancer, light on her feet. Aunt Peg remembered her grandmother, who we all knew as Nana, a proud Scot, had loved this dessert.

"What are the chances you would give me the recipe?" she asked the waitress.

"The chances are pretty good," she replied brightly, in her thick brogue, and she returned with a book of the hotel's recipes, pages protected by plastic, opened to Pavlova. My aunt copied the simple instructions onto a page in the small, spiral-topped notebook she kept in her purse for moments like this.

After we'd been home a few weeks, Aunt Peg and Uncle Jamie came to spend the weekend with me. We wanted to share photos and revisit some of the wonderful moments of our trip. For dinner, I had gone to some effort to find items we had enjoyed during our journey around the British Isles, including oat cakes and Stilton, steak and kidney pie, mashed potatoes and turnips ("tatties and neeps"), Whitbread beer and haggis, which had come home with me in a can. For dessert, I served Pavlova, heaped with fresh strawberries and whipped cream. "Oh, Nana!" Aunt Peg cried out, on first bite.

Ten years later, in Provence, Rosemary and I stayed in a little house in the tiny village of St. Roman de Malegarde. The house belonged to Rosemary's daughter and her husband, but they used it only as a rental. They lived in a larger house, up the lane. So we were neighbors for that short time.

St. Roman had only one small café, where we never ate, and no stores. We cooked for ourselves in the tiny kitchen of the house, which was very dark and attached to the rest of the houses on that lane. The mud walls were thick and there were few windows. If we needed supplies, we could drive to the larger town of Tulette, which was probably three or four miles away.

St. Roman is surrounded by vineyards, most of them above the village, and in the mornings I used to walk up into the vineyards where mostly old men were pruning the vines in the early mist. It was February, early spring in that part of France and there were the bright neon colors of the primrose blooming in courtyards and many of the almond trees had begun to blossom. After my walk to the vineyard, I sometimes took the bike and rode to Tulette. It was still early and Rosemary tended to sleep late. The road was relatively flat and the traffic very light so I felt as though I were flying through the open countryside. I recall a very distinct feeling of freedom as I peddled past the fields. Sometimes a man working in one of the vineyards would look up and wave, making me feel a part.

Like many of these towns, Tulette had market day on Tuesdays. Vendors came from various places to sell cheeses and fresh vegetables and sausages. Flowers. Olives. Their display was better than any still life I could think of. The foods were heaped into big wicker baskets and small chalkboards set among the produce identified the items and stated the prices. These vendors set up every day in one of the area towns, so if we missed Tuesday in Tulette, we could drive farther to one of the other towns on Wednesday or Thursday. Rosemary's daughter had a schedule to guide us. But we never missed market day in Tulette, though we often went to the bigger bazaar in Vaison. I should say, also, there was a wonderful variety of olive oils available.

But if I took the bike to Tulette, any day of the week, I could go to the bakery that sold fresh breads and croissants. You had to get there early or else they would sell out. So my bike ride had a mission: the earlier I went, the better chance I had of getting a croissant and a fresh loaf of bread to bring home for later.

This all took place in the early part of the year 2000. Only a few months prior, everyone had been waiting for the world to spin out of control as the big wheels of the world's calendar turned. There was a lot of futuristic talk of Y2K. Nostrodamus's predictions were often mentioned. Rosemary had been reading to me a lot about the forecasts of these prophets and how the clocks would stop on all computers and our electronic universe, so recently created, would come to an end. For Christmas, I had given Rosemary a "Y2K Survival Kit" that contained candles, an oil lamp and a bottle of lamp oil, matches, a pair of heavy socks and a scarf, and a rosary. It was kind of a joke. But not entirely. And, of course, nothing happened so we all felt a little relieved.

But, indeed, there were to be changes, astrological or otherwise. At home, before flying to France, I had left my house,
half-finished, or not even half, but torn apart and in the midst of
reassembly, and when I returned, I was greeted with the news that
my job with *Yankee*, which I had held for more than twenty years,
had been eliminated. Any further work would be done by the
piece. The aftershocks of that quake are still being felt. But that
was still in the future, as were the events of 9-11, which were well
more than a year away. And so, as I rode to Tulette that morning, anticipating the taste of the big chocolate croissant, I was, in
a sense, a bit of an innocent. I felt, in so many ways, that all was
right with the world.

Maybe I would have been charmed by the simplicity of
Tulette at any time during the 20th century. All the buildings in
the villages in Provence have stoic stone fronts and are connected,
like medieval fortresses huddled in expectation of the invasion of
the barbarians. The Huns seemed to have left a permanent mark
on this part of the world. The charm was in its antiquity and, even
in the relatively new world of New England, this is what people
come for, the nostalgic longing for a return to that innocence. In
Tulette I experienced that sweet return by parking my bike beside
the boulangerie and pushing open one half of the narrow double
door. A small bell jingled. The little store smelled of sugar and
fresh crusts. Behind the counter was a display of cakes, gaudy in
turquoise and bright yellow and pink.

"Bon jour!" The slight woman behind the counter sang her
two-note greeting. Few in this part of France spoke English and
so I had to rely on my shallow language skills. *"Bon jour!"* I sang

in return and ordered the croissant, *avec chocolat,* and a loaf of the *pain frais.* There were just a few left. As well, I ordered *thé* and picked up an *International Herald Tribune.* The woman took pains to wrap both the bun and the bread in white paper and tie each, expertly knotting the string, which I would momentarily, or sooner, untie.

The air outside was still cool but I craved it. At home in New Hampshire, the snowbanks were still high. And so I took my purchases out to the small table just outside the door. I sat down on the wrought-iron chair and worked open the skillfully wrapped package, spreading the stiff paper out on the table. A few knowing pigeons came to seek. I broke the large pastry in half. The aroma of the chocolate rose to settle me. The first bite sent a flurry of pastry flakes, which drifted onto the front of my sweater and onto the paper before me. The buttery creation melted in my mouth. The pigeons waddled around at my feet, hoping.

I opened the newspaper and browsed the headlines, but the news seemed somehow otherworldly and I felt very disconnected from it. I wanted to save part of the croissant for Rosemary and so I wrapped it back in the paper, retying the string, though not in the artful way it had been presented to me. It all seemed delicious, the tastes of the air and the pastry. Even in the chill, I sat there for the longest time, drinking in the beauty of Tulette along with the very last leaves of the tea.

At last, I put the croissant and the newspaper into the basket that hung off the handlebars of the bike and peddled back to St. Roman, to see if Rosemary was up yet.

Pavlova
(adapted from the Argyle Arms, Lochgilphead, Scotland)

4 egg whites
1 cup castor (superfine) sugar
1 teaspoon white vinegar
1 teaspoon vanilla
1 teaspoon cornflour (cornstarch)

Beat the egg whites (add a pinch of salt) until stiff. Continue beating, gradually adding the sugar, vinegar and vanilla until the mixture is thick. Lightly fold in the cornstarch. Pile it all into a lightly greased pie plate. Smooth it up the sides of the plate, leaving a dip in the center for any filling you might choose to add after it's baked. Bake at 250 degrees for an hour and a half. Or, for a crisper edge, bake at 400 degrees for five minutes and then turn the oven down to 250 degrees for an hour and a half. I find this is really good with fresh fruit added after the crust cools. And, of course, whipped cream. Serves 6.

The Kitchen at Mary's Farm

WHEN I FIRST BOUGHT this farm, in 1997, the house was configured oddly, mostly because it had been a farm since 1762 and the house and its barns had gradually evolved in very humble ways to what it was at the time of my purchase. Only three families had lived here in that long time. Most recently the house had belonged to Mary Walker. She and her family had lived in the house and farmed the land since 1946, and it's through Mary that the place had become known about town and in the vernacular as Mary's farm. I have a photo of the house, probably taken when it was for sale in the 1940s so I have a rough idea of how it looked at that time.

Most of the additions to the house involved the barn. Like many New England farms, an extension of various sheds and add-ons stretched from the house to the barn, thus making a pass-through that could allow the farmer and his family to get to the barn and feed the animals in the winter without having to shovel a path or wade through drifts of snow. Since this farm was at one time threatened by plans for a major highway that would pass right through the farm's south fields, an intensive study of this farm had been done, as it is likely one of the oldest farms, if not the oldest, in the region. The historical significance of this farm as well as other places in this vicinity apparently helped to defeat the highway proposal, which would have cut a wide and noisy swath through this peaceful place. That it might have been otherwise makes me so grateful, but it is an odd kind of gratitude. If the highway had gone through, I would not be here. But the fact that it was proposed and resulted in such an unholy ruckus around here has enriched my understanding and knowledge of Mary's farm. My gratitude, then, is for all that might have been but is not.

Paul and I owned the barn that adjoined Mary's farm. At one time long ago, the barn had been a hay barn for the Willards, who preceded the Walkers in owning the farm. We had made the old barn into a satisfying workplace for both of us. Paul had his carpentry shop there and I had an office from which I wrote every day. So we already had a tiny piece of Mary's farm and were thus on the periphery of the highway fight, which went on for many years.

The big house, which now resembles a sinking ship as it leans into the hill, seems to have started out, back in the days just following the French and Indian War, as a small Cape and expanded in various ways, including a rather mysterious lower level that was basement on one side and ground floor on the other. This was where the kitchen was when I bought the farm — in the very back of the house, likely created out of one of the shed add-ons.

We sometimes came up to visit Mary and, like everyone else who ever came to this house, we entered into the kitchen. Until the farm went up for sale after Mary's death, this was the only room of the house I'd ever been in.

I've been told that the well that the family once used is under the floorboards of the old kitchen, which is pretty convincing evidence that, at one time, the house did not extend that far back. In any case, Mary's kitchen was a welcoming place that included a small kitchen area, with counter and simple appliances, a table and chairs and then it opened out to a kind of living room. At the back of the room was a fireplace and Mary and her sister could often be found in chairs near the hearth. Mary's kitchen was not much in terms of appliances or counter space, but she somehow managed to sustain a catering business. She was a well-known cook (as well as gardener) and apparently brought forth all kinds of wonderful dishes from this humble place. Since we were right next door for a number of years and passed by on our way home from work, I recall that the only lights we ever saw on were in that area of the house. It was as if they lived in that one small space of this otherwise rambling house.

Buying this farm remains, to me, one of the most daring chapters of my life, not much different from what it would have been if I'd suddenly married a man of questionable repute in the belief I could change his ways. After that almost completely impetuous act, the first thing I had to do was plot out how I would change the house. I think at the very first, I believed it could be as it was and I could figure out how to live in it, perhaps in the same way that Mary and her sister did, by restricting my life to a small area. But the one galvanizing factor about the house, likely what had attracted me to it in the first place and also what made it a place the neighborhood thought worth saving, was the view.

The view from Mary's farm is a dramatic, up-close look at Mount Monadnock, the long ridges that lead to the summit stretching out on either side. It's the full view of the mountain. I sometimes call it the "full monty" as it seems like all of it is exposed, nothing hidden. As the crow flies, the mountain is about six miles from the front window and, thanks to all my forward-thinking neighbors present and past, the land that we all look at is preserved from development for all time. And so, at night, there are no lights visible from my house, just the solemn, peaceful dark hump of the big hill. The view and its wild surroundings — once home to wolves and now to coyotes — were why I came here. While living in the back kitchen, it disappointed me greatly to discover that in order to enjoy the view, I had to walk outside.

The other wonderful aspect of the house was its siting: facing due south on the high hill, the house has incredible solar potential, which, with its small or nonexistent windows and time-darkened walls and floors, was underutilized, to say the least. And so, in thinking about what to do with the house, my one guiding vision was to orient the house toward the mountain and toward the sun. As it was, the kitchen, located at the north end of the house and with the old dark pine paneling, was a very dark and cold place.

I was immediately acquainted with the house's failings as the pipes froze and broke in that kitchen just two weeks after my purchase. I learned from the plumber who came to my rescue that

Mary and her sister spent winters in Florida, which eliminated the need to keep the pipes from freezing in winter. They simply drained them before they left. As well, the chimney where they had their cozy woodstove plugged in to the fireplace was condemned by the town fire chief. He came up one day and told me that there had been a fire in that chimney every year for ten years. I guess it was so predictable that "one year, the guys didn't want to be called out on New Year's Eve *again*, so one of them volunteered to come over here and babysit the chimney that night." He told me to never use it unless I had it rebuilt or lined. So much for warmth in the back of the kitchen.

That part of the house sat dead on the ground, no crawl space. It was just sitting on the ground. Since that whole section dates to the 1800s, I have no idea why it did not rot long ago. However, since it's still true and square, that was not a question I wanted to look into very deeply. Let sleeping dogs lie. But the fact that it sat on the ground contributed a lot to the fact that, for me, Mary's old kitchen became a relentlessly cold place.

Upstairs, however, in the front part of the house where I could gaze out at the mountain, had the benefit of the oil burner and so was warm, or could be warm. There was a big old living room up there on one side of the stairway and two bedrooms on the other side. The house had seven bedrooms when I bought it. I didn't need that many bedrooms and, since, to some degree, our taxes are calculated on number of bedrooms, I certainly wanted to eliminate some of them. Up there, I could see the big old living room as the kitchen and those two bedrooms as a big dining room. Like all old houses, each room and every section of the house was walled off and separated by doors. The work started immediately. As I took up residence in the old, cold kitchen downstairs, walls and doors were removed from that area of the upstairs, where it was warm and, as the walls came down, saturated with sunlight. When all was done, I could say I did many things to this house and made many changes, but the one thing I did that was the most important was that I let in the light, which gave the house life and dimension that isn't possible to create from wood or plaster.

I wanted the kitchen to have the same elements of the other kitchens I had created in the other old houses I'd had the privilege to live in — long enough to bring them back from the brink. I wanted the open shelves where I could show off my collection of bowls and pitchers and I wanted good solid handmade cabinets. A sink that felt in keeping with the age of the house. A big pantry. And a place for my wood cookstove and the big old Glenwood gas range, which had become the useful pair I'd kept going for so long. And a big space for a good-sized table and chairs — room for at least six people to sit around the table comfortably. I had no intention of making this a kitchen for one. That big old living room lent itself to all of that and so the work began on the new kitchen, which was to be warm and facing the mountain.

To create the pantry, we had to take out the stairway that led to the upstairs. The bedrooms upstairs had to be gutted because of severe damage done by a previous tenant. And so, for the time being, we sealed off access to the third floor. All I really wanted was that kitchen. The greatest heartache of leaving the house in Chesham was that I had to part with the kitchen Paul had created for me there, at a time when he was very ill and, as it turned out, near death. To my eyes, the room had a beauty far beyond its physical attributes. Perhaps the oddest thing about buying this house and redoing it was my choice of carpenter to perform the work. I chose my ex-husband, Michael.

For any woman alone, it is especially hard to discern who you can trust when it comes to hiring work. Many carpenters, when working for a single woman, seem to become involved with them romantically. Around here, that seems to be a trend. I couldn't imagine a less inviting prospect and certainly one fraught with possible complications and repercussions. I was not interested in that kind of relationship, only good work performed to a satisfying conclusion. I had an electrician who had done all my work in all my houses and I had a plumber as well. These wonderful men had always come through for me. But the carpentry stumped me. I was a bit spoiled as Michael had done the work on the early houses and then Paul on the later. My early relationship with Michael lacked many things, but one area where Michael and I really communicated well was on building and houses. In a sense, we spoke the same language. Certainly we had grown up together in this way, learning the trade side by side by reading books and talking with architects and, most of all, from Michael's uncle Johnny, a contractor on Long Island who came up to help us at least twice on that first house we built. And after Paul's death, Michael and I had reconciled. He had married again and then divorced, again. Approaching midlife, Michael seemed to be coming into a more introspective place and he sometimes stopped by to say hello and have a cup of coffee. And so, when I bought Mary's farm, I called him for advice. I knew he would be honest with me. I was asking for quotes from other area builders and the range was expansive. And expensive. I asked him to make a bid as well.

It went from there. Over the course of nearly ten years, Michael and his very able assistant, Henri, helped me rebuild every part of this house. There is just one room that has not been changed, redone or eliminated altogether. I never thought that the house would be so completely renovated. Like taking out a row when knitting a sweater, it's really hard to stop once you start. It just keeps unraveling until it's back to the beginning.

The kitchen came first but, in so many ways, it was and is the most prideful part of all. When I first sketched what I wanted on a small piece of paper, I had not envisioned the light that would enter the house once the walls and doors came down, nor had I envisioned the cheerful welcome of the painted floors and walls that would bring color and its own kind of light to my life. I had not envisioned the unusual life that would take shape here and inhabit the farm in its own unique way. And while I was drawing the plans and choosing things like cabinet hardware and sink faucets, I forgot to imagine the smell of good food that would rise up from my stoves, to feed my friends whenever they would come to see me.

Beef Stew

This has become my favorite winter recipe. My wood cookstove is ideally suited for stews and so I make this a lot during the winter. I set it on the back of the stove and let it simmer throughout the day.

3 pounds beef, chuck or top round, cut into generous cubes

2 tablespoons flour

2 tablespoons olive oil

3 medium-sized potatoes, peeled and cut into quarters

3 medium-sized onions, peeled and cut into quarters

1 pound carrots, peeled and cut into 2-inch lengths

1 pound parsnips, peeled and cut into chunks

12 black olives

6 cloves garlic

1 bay leaf

⅓ cup tomato paste

2 cups red wine

1 tablespoon balsamic vinegar

1 teaspoon salt

fresh ground pepper

Dredge the beef cubes in flour, coating thoroughly. Heat the olive oil in a skillet and sear the cubes quickly in the hot oil. Remove and place in a large stainless-steel or cast-iron pot — a Dutch oven is ideal. Add the vegetables, olives, garlic and bay leaf. Spread the tomato paste across the veggies with a rubber spatula. Pour in the wine and the vinegar. Sprinkle the salt over everything and grind a generous amount of fresh pepper over all. Cover and place over medium heat till the juices bubble. Keep it at a slow simmer for 2 to 3 hours or until the meat is fork-tender. Alternatively you can put this in the oven at 350 degrees and simmer it for the same amount of time. (You can also do this in your slow cooker at low heat, for 6 to 8 hours, or at high heat for 3 to 5.) Serves 6.

Cooking for One

I've been alone a long time now, nearly twenty years. It's something I never imagined and yet at this point in my life, I can't imagine it being otherwise. I guess you could say I've grown accustomed to this life alone. I've figured it out.

My life alone intensified when, five years after Paul died, both my parents died and some time later, my aunt Peg and uncle Jamie left this world as well. It is sobering to be this alone in the world. Being without a spouse, without parents and without children leaves one in a kind of dangling solitude for which there truly is no rescue. It is simply a state of being. And I figured I could continue feeling at the end of that perilous rope or I could find a family of my own, a family that does not have the traditional ties but one which, nevertheless, provides all of what the traditional family provides and, in many many cases, probably much more. So one thing I figured out was that I had the benefit of being able to choose this family.

A lot of the rest of what I figured out has to do with food. I realized, perhaps first with my suppers with Rosemary, that by inviting someone to join me for dinner — in some cases, that "someone" can be as many as twenty-one people — I've accomplished a lot. I love to cook, so I have brought people to my home for whom I can cook. I love having people in my life — and this provides that as well. And I can presume that I've been able to provide these people with some good food and company as well. Though I cannot be absolutely certain I've done that for them, I can be certain about the pleasure it brings me.

It's a mystery to me why I haven't remarried. I suppose there are many reasons, but I do recall that in those first confusing months after Paul's death, I felt certain I would marry again. I had been married twice and it seemed like a natural state to me. In my marriage to Paul, I had been so happy and so I reasoned that I would find that again. I wished we had had children but life is so complex and for those who truly believe that everything in one's life is a result of a deliberate decision, I can only say I wish that were really true. Most of what any of us encounter is such a complex stew of circumstance and happenstance, we're truly fortunate if we can choose what we'll have for dinner that night, much less our own destiny. Anything further that seems deliberate is simply illusion. Paul was thirty-nine when he died. I have many friends who have lost their spouses at a young age and I know people whose children have died. I have friends who have had accidents in which they have lost their legs or their minds. I know people who like to believe that if something tragic happens to someone else, they have, in some way, brought this on themselves. I think this makes them feel better, making such devastating shifts in one's life within our control. No, it seems to me that in many cases we are asked to react to circumstances, not choose them.

For whatever reason, I am still alone — but I'm not alone. Not in any real way. For one thing, the renovation of this house consumed me, as would have any marriage with at least three children. There were decisions to be made constantly, budgets to be balanced, supplies to be picked up or delivered, and all for the ultimate well-being of the structure as well as my soul. I *needed* this house in a way I had never needed anything. I'm not sure I felt that way when I bought it, as the decision to buy had come about very rapidly and could have been called, should have been called, impulsive. The farm had gone up for sale very suddenly and developers were pushing in. It needed to be saved and the neighbors had banded together to accomplish that. Two weeks before, I had not even thought of selling my home in Chesham and buying Mary's farm. But that is what happened and the faith of my neighbors spurred me on. I needed to do this for them and for the community, as well as for myself. Again, it was not a single voice, but the force of the group. Without that, the whole farm might have gone into development would have vastly changed this road, this town, and, on a broader scale, the complexion of New England as a rural place with beauty and peace.

After I bought, the pace of the project quickened, and once the first few boards were torn from the side of the house, the pace didn't slow for ten long years. And so, inside that storm of activity, I found a compelling heart to each and every one of my days, a rhythm that kept beating and never slowed until just recently. Now still unfinished but so close, I can rest a bit and reflect. For a long time, reflection was not possible. Or even desirable. You could say it was a kind of frenzy, which, if set to fast motion, as is popular now with house-building shows, you would see siding and roofs fly off, additions and dormers magically appear, walls disappear, doors move from one opening to another, and windows vanish as new windows zoom into place. If Mary were to come back from the dead for a visit, she would be lost in her own house.

But within all of that, there was always time for a meal. The first really new part of this house was the kitchen and the dining room. And so these two spaces became almost sacred as other spaces were pounded into place. And there were meals, gatherings, parties, something for which I was not particularly well prepared. My aunt Peg gave dinner parties on occasion and, as a child, I sat there uncomfortably as the erudite conversation wafted high above my head. But the food was good. That was always something to look forward to. And there was something else, something much harder to grasp. The dining room in that old Colonial house had a big fireplace and in the winter, the fire was always lit, as were the candles, which gave the room a glow and a cozy feeling, as if we had all come in out of the cold to gather there. Of course, we had, in a sense, but there was something more primeval about it to my way of thinking, a kind of bonding together against the rigors of the wilderness of an evermore confusing world. Maybe, in some really vague way, that is what I'm reaching for when I invite friends for dinner.

My first bit of fortune came with the table that was left to me by my parents. It had belonged to my great-grandparents. My great-grandparents, I should say, had a lot of money, money that never made it past the year 1929. But, oh, before that time, they lived high and happily within a grand home that had formal gardens, servants' quarters and a darkroom for my grandfather's hobby. When the stock market fell, the money was gone but the furniture stayed with us, passed down and down into ever smaller homes. In our modest house in New Jersey, the table had been a circle with four rather grand chairs around it. Two of these chairs had arms and, with their high ornate backs, the chairs seemed somehow out of scale with the table, which had a beautiful mahogany finish and a grand base carved into eagle's claws grasping big wooden balls.

As a child, I loved to hide under the table and was always slightly awed by the fierce nature of what held up this table — and with what appeared to grip the rug. In the basement, my father had stored four more chairs to match the set and four leaves that could be set into the expanding table frame. I had never seen it with more than one leaf in it because my parents' dining room had been too small. But once the table made its way to this new house, I was able to expand it completely and set all the chairs around it. I had already envisioned it many times as the two old bedrooms were being demolished and the new wainscoting put into place. This would be where the table would be. This would be where the fun would be.

The appearance of my new dining room and the banquet-sized table must have seemed absurd to anyone watching this process, because this was a home for one person. Who was going to sit around this table? I'm sure it's a question on the lips of anyone who comes in this house, especially all the men who came to do various jobs, wiring and plumbing and flooring. I could see them glance into the big room and then glance again.

It began some years back when, weary of trying to figure out what to do for holidays like Thanksgiving and Christmas, I hit on the idea of what I called "orphan holidays." Gradually I noticed that I was not the only one around who was alone at Christmas. There were others, in fact; not only were there those who were truly alone, as Rosemary was at that time in her life, but there were others who were not technically alone but in transition: friends whose spouses had recently died, friends in the midst of divorce, friends in some other kind of despair and simply friends who did not have family nearby — or who had family they did not enjoy. I realized we could all come together on that day and it fulfilled the need in me to cook a big meal for many hungry friends. At the most, I've crowded twenty-five people around that table (with an extension) and at the least, I've hosted seven, who were just as grateful for a good place to go to share what can otherwise be a deadly day of remorse or sadness while (you are certain) the entire rest of the world is happily celebrating with their big families. An exaggeration, of course, as I know there are people with large families who grit their teeth through the whole ordeal but, truly, holidays can be so difficult for anyone alone.

As well, some time ago, I started another tradition that I observe every few years. I noticed, at one point, that I have an extraordinary number of friends with birthdays in February. I guess I started noticing when I was having to buy out the card store every year at that time. It prompted me to think of giving one great big party for all of them, whether they knew each other or not. And so I did. Once again, there were more people than could fit around my table — a couple of late January people edged in. We all crowded around the table, dined on roast lamb and celebrated the joy of knowing each other and passing another year together. One year, we had three people celebrating their seventieth birthdays, two people celebrating their fiftieth and one who was turning twenty-five. A complete celebration of the cycle of life.

I love this as a way to try out new recipes and for the joy of bringing out old favorites. I also love it as a way of loving my house. You could look at it as something very similar to loving to get dressed up, that wonderful dress just hanging in the closet, waiting for the right occasion. Well, I love dressing up my house. It's a chance to decorate (I never even got out a single ornament before I started giving the orphan Christmases. It seemed so pointless. Decorate for what? For whom?) and to use the good china and silverware, a chance to change the tablecloth, put new candles into the candlesticks, use the gravy boat. Whatever. It's no different from what everyone else loves about having the family to their house for Christmas. It's a chance to change gears, see the house through different eyes. My favorite moment of all is at the height of the party, to sit for a moment and listen, listen to the talk, the laughter, the joy inside these walls that are, for most of the rest of the time, silent as a mosque.

I love every part of a party: the planning of the menu, the cleaning of the house, the setting of the table, the cooking of the meal, which I insist must be almost completely ready before the first guest arrives. All I want to have to do once the party starts is to put the food on the table. After all, I want to attend this party. It's why I'm giving it!

And so, out of the somber puzzle of how to cook for one came the joyous process of cooking for twenty and more. I highly recommend it.

Here are some tips for giving a big party:

• Don't make things you have never made before. Be certain of what you will be serving. You can afford to be a bit adventurous but don't try out that "foolproof" soufflé for the first time for the big party. Save that one for yourself and a friend. Have a list of some of your favorite and tastiest dishes and choose those that are complimentary flavors. Be sure you can expand the recipe easily enough.

• Clean the house a couple of days before the party. Yes, the house will be a complete mess when the party is over and you will have to clean it all over again. Save the really thorough cleaning for after the party. But don't lean to the old wisdom of not cleaning before a party because it's going to be a mess within hours. You want to show your house off.

• Set the table the day before. By then you will know who is coming, so you know how many settings to put out, and you will know the theme (birthday, Christmas, a specific celebration like graduation). You can, if you want, add some simple decorations to augment. But remember that the table needs to be somewhat clear so food can flow around the table. Don't overdo the decorations. Less is more. Flowers are nice but be sure you choose low arrangements in the center. People need to be able to see everyone around the table without flowers blocking their view. Add candles as you wish. If you can have the table lit by candles, it gives the event a very special feeling.

- Plan the guest list carefully. If you have friends you think would enjoy some other friends who they've not yet met, a dinner party is a great opportunity to get them together. If you have friends who do not get along, include only one or the other. It doesn't happen often, but if you don't take care with the guest list, a party can become a powder keg. Pay close attention to everyone's religious and political devotions!

- When you invite your guests, be sure to ask them if they have allergies or dietary preferences and make note. My aunt Peg kept a card file on all her friends' likes and dislikes and that was in a day when you didn't expect anyone to disavow the eating of meat. I don't keep a file but I try to remember what's what with my friends, and if I don't know, I always ask. This avoids someone going hungry or, worst of all, a party where anyone doesn't have a good time.

- After you know who can eat what, plan the menu at least a week in advance. Be sure you have taken into account everyone's needs (this can be challenging but fun) and balance the menu accordingly.

- Be sure you have all the ingredients you need in hand twenty-four hours ahead.

- Have anything that can be made in advance, like pies or certain salads, prepared the night before.

- Have a checklist of everything you need to do and to prepare. Try to make the list in order of what needs to be done first and last. Check things off as you go. This cuts down on last minute panic.

- One hour before guests are to arrive, you should have just about everything done. Plan it that way. Then go and take a shower and get dressed. You don't want to be caught in your apron with your hair askew when everyone arrives. It's all about planning. And, remember, this party is for you to enjoy as much as for your guests.

- Delegate. If there is a roast to be carved or wine bottles to be opened, have in mind a couple of your friends who you can ask to take care of this when they arrive. If you are alone, you have to get used to asking for help. That was a hard lesson for me to learn.

- Be sure to have a variety of drinks available. If budget is a consideration, don't serve hard liquor. It's more expensive than beer or wine, which most people drink, and requires other accoutrements (ice, mixers, lemons and limes). But be sure to have several choices for those who do not drink — seltzer water and some kind of juice usually cover the bases. It's important to have available what you think your guests want. If you don't drink, don't impose that stricture on your guests. You have invited them to come and enjoy themselves and that implies that you want to make them happy in the style to which they are accustomed.

- Put all drinks and hors d'oeuvres out on a selected table beforehand, with napkins, glasses, corkscrew, whatever is needed, so guests can help themselves. Make all this as automatic as possible. And have that set up in advance. As people arrive, you can simply invite them to help themselves to a drink of their choice.

• Pace the courses. Don't rush the meal. Make sure there is plenty of food so that guests can have seconds if they want.

• Be sure to have some kind of coffee or tea (caffeine) available when the meal has ended.

• You are there to enjoy yourself but you are also there to make sure all your guests are happy. If you notice that one of your guests is, for some reason, hanging back or not included, pull her into the conversation deliberately, but be subtle.

• The reason for the party will usually dictate the size of the crowd, but I've always felt that a dinner party for eight is the ideal size. It's easy to cook for that number and the conversation is much calmer and more focused when eight gather around a table.

A DINNER PARTY FOR EIGHT
For a Spring Evening

SAMPLE MENU
Cold Cucumber Soup
Roast Lamb
Mint Pesto or Maharaja's Chutney
Steamed Asparagus with Hollandaise
Orange Couscous
Rhubarb Pie

Cold Cucumber Soup

I love this recipe. I often make it for myself on hot days. It's very low in calories and very refreshing on hot nights. I make it in the blender and keep it in the refrigerator for several nights' worth of refreshment. I also use it often when entertaining because it can be made ahead of time and kept in the refrigerator until the party begins. A soup course makes a dinner party just that much more special.

4 cups cucumber, peeled, seeded and cut into small pieces

2 cups water

2 cups plain yogurt

2 cloves garlic

½ cup fresh mint leaves

1 tablespoon honey

1½ teaspoons salt

1 teaspoon dried dill weed

Puree everything in the blender. Refrigerate for several hours before serving, garnished with a cross of small mint leaves. Serve 6.

My Favorite Recipe, Today

THERE'S A FABLE that goes 'round up here from time to time. The story took root about a hundred years ago, in the next town. The selectmen were apparently contacted and asked to do something about a woman everyone thought had gone crazy. And so the selectmen talked with her husband, who took offense and replied that he couldn't think of anything she might have seen that could have made her crazy. "She hasn't been out of the kitchen in twenty years," he reasoned.

In our global reality, food embraces the world. Even in recent times, only thirty years ago, a good pizza was hard to find in northern New England and now there is variety enough to please anyone from anywhere in the world. Maybe if I were thirty years younger, coming here, I would not have seen the need to find a way to make a good pizza. But it wouldn't have been half as much fun and I wouldn't have my proud creation to show for it.

The kitchen is only the start of it. The rest is how it's all put together and for whom. One man who writes beautifully about food, John Thorne, claims to like best to cook for himself. Cooking, he writes, is "an act of not just love but of loving. We come closest to feeling this when we cook just for ourselves. The more others intrude, the more complex and confusing the calculus; turned loose in the kitchen alone, we feel an intimate connection that seems almost illicitly intense, exactly why so many won't cook for themselves at all."

What he says seems to me to be the reverse of what any woman would say. The perspective of a man who cooks is, by nature, drastically different from that of a woman who, at one time, was expected to spend much of her time in the kitchen and to produce reasonably palatable meals (and try not to go crazy). Even though times have changed and we no longer make the mistake of assuming that a woman cooks and a man does not, there are certain truths that persist. Mostly, even now, the women do the cooking and, willing or not, loving it or not, we spend a lot of time in the kitchen. These times, for most women, are not "illicitly intense," but rather comfortable communion in a place that has a permanent and welcome "intimate connection."

One day last fall, I was trying to sort through the contents of some boxes that had been left to me. One of the boxes contained poems and short stories that my grandmother had written. I had stored them in the upstairs of one of the barns here and when I encountered them, I was alarmed to find that mice or perhaps squirrels had gotten into the boxes and chewed up some of the pages. They might as well have nibbled off little pieces of my heart. I sat down on a bench. The hay loft doors were open and there was a pleasant breeze coming in, enough to rustle the pages as I sat there for some long time, reading.

At last, as the breeze turned chill, I organized the pieces in the best way that I could and resettled them into a new plastic storage bin I had bought in anticipation of this task. At the very bottom of the old box, which seemed to be disintegrating as fast as I unpacked it, I found one more thing, a thick pad of light blue paper with handwriting on it. I brought this into the light and recognized the blue ink as my grandmother's handwriting. "Mrs. Stockwell's Cake," she wrote at the top and there was the recipe, carefully spelling out the ingredients for this cake, which I had never heard of or tasted. I lifted to the next page and there was another, this one for "Cocoanut Cake." And another beneath that for "Brandied Peaches," which I do remember hearing my father pine for. And so it went for about fifty pages. I paged through the entire pad of recipes, few of them familiar to me, either personally or universally. Spanish Cream, Snow Cake and Jelly Cake. Coffee Jelly and Coffee Mousse. Sponge Cake, Bread Cake and Composition Cake. The handwriting was faded by age and was hard in some cases to decipher. In other places, she measures things in primitive ways, by the tumbler, as in "2 tumblers of milk" or by the goblet (is there a difference, I wondered?). And elsewhere she measures by the spoon as in, "one spoon of baking soda."

At first it looked like I had unearthed a long-hidden family treasure but then there was this possibly insurmountable gap in time, a stop time of sorts. One of the pages is dated 1894. And they all seem to have been written at once, with the same pen, as if preparing a manuscript. Perhaps she was. But, like this long-lost pad of recipes, her cooking never quite trickled down, but instead stayed in the trunk with other unpublished manuscripts. Other than the Brandied Peaches, which calls for five pints of "white brandy," none of these recipes rang any bells with me.

Should they have? I don't know who Mrs. Stockwell was and my grandmother never made that cake for me, so would it be anything more than an interesting exercise for me to try out that recipe? I doubt it. Unfortunately, perhaps, there is a cliché about all of us treasuring our grandmother's recipes. I'm sure this is the case for many, but not for all. Not for me. Maybe the chain stopped with my mother's disinterest in food, but stop it did. And a different, more contemporary chain started. So many times, the connections matter more than the taste.

I see now that my cooking has been an evolution, an eclectic mix of not only recipes but of places I've been and the various people who have affected my life. Aunt Peg. Marge and Skip, as well as the places and the age in which I lived. Necessarily, food goes with us wherever we go, evolves with us and our needs in the same way that our faces and our bodies change as we age.

I have no idea where the next decades will take me in or out of the kitchen, but today my favorite recipe is from a recipe card I picked up in a natural-food store in North Carolina, probably twenty years ago. I made it first for some food-loving Southern friends. It took me fifteen minutes to make. We scraped the bowl and longed for more. I brought the recipe home with me and made it again and again, each time adjusting the ingredients until it was just the way I liked it.

For nine long years, I lived in my unfinished house as it took shape around me. At times during the renovations, I've had a bed in almost every room of this house, moving from one room to the next as the action circled around me. At the end of each day, sawdust settling, I hunted around for dinner. As you can tell from the recipes in this book, I love slow food but during that time of renovation, "fast food" appealed to me. The frenzy of the project prompted me to start collecting recipes like this one that could be fixed in a hurry, but which were (key point) delicious and nutritious. This dish was certainly all of that and more. It's great on a summer night but I love it warm, too. The sweetness of the orange and the currants, the tang of the vinegar and the gentle nature of the couscous, soft as a cloud, make it almost a whole food. But coupled with meat from the grill, it's a meal worthy of an updated version of Peg Bracken's *I Hate to Cook Book*.

Unconsciously, then, my unfinished house, which is now (almost!) finished, made me into a fan of fast foods. By the time you read this, I might not be making Orange Couscous anymore, but that's just the way it is when it comes to the fluid, unbounded, fickle world of food and those of us who love to eat.

Orange Couscous

1½ cups orange juice

½ cup water

⅓ cup canola oil

2 tablespoons white vinegar

squeeze of fresh lemon

1 teaspoon salt

1 teaspoon honey

1 teaspoon cinnamon

2 cups couscous

¼ cup currants

½ cup red bell pepper, diced

grated orange zest

In a saucepan, bring the first eight ingredients to a boil, whisking once in a while. In a large serving bowl, mix together the couscous and the currants. Pour the hot liquid over the couscous and let steep for 10 to 15 minutes. When it's cool, fluff it up with a fork and add the peppers and the zest. Serve warm or cold. Serves 6.

Postscript

As I sort through my overfilled recipe book, I see that at times I have become almost obsessed with a certain recipe, making it over and over since it just tastes *sooo* good, and then a few years pass and I will come across the recipe and realize I haven't made it in ages. Like places we have lived or jobs we have had or people we have loved: they are, for a time, our reality. And then, for all kinds of reasons, we move on. We carry the recipes with us, layers that form us and become, in the most wonderful way, part of who we are. In their delectable nature, the foods of our lives can transport us to another place or into the company of someone we have loved. I can't make iced tea without thinking of my aunt Peg. I can't make rhubarb soup without thinking of my family in Iceland. Or Mushrooms Provençale without remembering those halcyon days in Brattleboro in the 1970s. Conversely, I can't make chicken and dumplings without thinking of Rosemary or of our neighbor Paul, neither of whom cook. But they like to eat. There are all kinds of reasons why we love the taste of things and only part of it is the actual recipe or the individual ingredients that comprise it. My pantry overflows with the bounty of a segmented, changing life that has transformed into a tasty homage to that part of my life and to those people who helped create it.

This organic flow of the food that makes up our lives is ongoing as we add to the repertoire and then dive back into our archives and find or revive recipes that once came around like clockwork until something new caught our fancy and supplanted the old. I suppose it's no different from the expanding repertoire of a performer, always finding new material but never really abandoning the old favorites. Just temporarily suspending them.

Indeed, our hunger is great, and not just for the meal. One day last winter, my neighbor fell and sustained injuries that landed her temporarily in a wheelchair. She lives alone, next door to me. Since there are only three houses, widely spaced, up on the top of this ridge, each one of us counts. We matter to each other. So as soon as she came home from the hospital, I put a chicken into the pot and started to make chicken pie. I'd acquired the recipe years ago while doing a story for *Yankee* about a woman whose chicken pies were the centerpiece of the town suppers, which raised money for the volunteer fire company — the fire engine that chicken pie bought. I loved the recipe and made it so often I feared my friends had tired of it and moved on. But when someone needs not only food but comfort, I instinctively revive the chicken pie. This was just such a time, when I knew that the meal would be not only delicious but also soothing, something that could nourish her on more levels than just the simple one of sustenance.

It was the first of many dinners we shared with each other. In the course of that meal, and the others that followed, we got caught up. We hadn't seen each other in a while and there was news to share, even though she was in pain and in the first stage of processing what had happened to her. Her accident, while unfortunate and bleak in many ways, brought us together when we had been otherwise too busy to find time to share a meal. Her new circumstance made us slow down and pay attention.

I was to find that in the days that followed, I was sometimes not the first one to the door with my portable meal — other friends from town were beating me to it. So we organized a system where we knew that she would have a meal brought to her at the end of each day. Who knows whether it was the food or the company of friends — sometimes better than medication — that came along with the basket. Like my friend Rosemary, as she approached Communion, *I want it all.* While the chicken stewed, the house filled with that familiar aroma that does as much to comfort me as it does those who receive the resulting concoction. Food is an adventure, food is communion, food is comfort, food is love. Food is a very big way that we live our lives. We might as well make it good.

About the Author

E DIE CLARK has been a writer and editor of books and magazines for the past thirty-five years. She has written extensively about New England in award-winning feature stories for *Yankee* magazine, where she served as Senior Editor, Fiction Editor and Senior Writer for twenty-four years. She is now Contributing Editor to that magazine and others. In her hundreds of published articles, she has written about food, travel and personalities as well as controversial issues such as Lyme disease, land development and water pollution. Her memoir, *The Place He Made*, about her husband's death from cancer, was described by the *New York Times Book Review* as "a triumph of the human spirit [which] may take its quiet place among the best of the literature." She has been a fellow at the MacDowell Colony and at Hedgebrook Writers Colony, as well as a visiting writer at Northern Michigan University. She has taught in the MFA program at Emerson College and frequently conducts workshops. An earlier collection, *The View from Mary's Farm*, has received generous acclaim. To learn more about her work, visit www.edieclark.com.

Praise for *The View from Mary's Farm*

Edie Clark is a transporting writer—gifted with a keen eye, a wide heart, and a transcending faith in soil, sky, and stars. Impeccably honest and deeply moving, *The View from Mary's Farm* reaffirms the power of place in the lives of those who dare to live life fully.

— **Beth Kephart**, *author of* Ghosts in the Garden

When known things are so deeply felt, as they are in this collection, they acquire a wonderful strangeness, richer than new things, just learned.

— **Arturo Vivante**, *author of* Solitude and Other Stories

Open this volume of a fine author's work, so that you may view her house and gardens, the surprises of sky and steadfastness of the land, which have become her art, her reason to be.

— **Carolyn Chute**, *author of* The Beans of Egypt, Maine

Moose, snow, roses, rhubarb are among the many points of departure for Edie Clark as she engages questions of history, community, and the natural world in the essays collected here. Each one is to be treasured for its wit and insight, and for its clear, graceful prose. Taken together, these pieces illuminate a world in its complex entirety. *The View from Mary's Farm* stands as a fine measure of Clark's years of accomplishment.

— **Jane Brox**, *author of* Clearing Land

To order copies of this book or *The View from Mary's Farm,* go to **www.edieclark.com** or send a check or money order for $18.95 ($14.95 plus $4 shipping and handling) to:

> Mary's Farm
> P.O. Box 112
> Dublin, NH 03444

For information on bulk orders and publisher's discounts, go to **www.edieclark.com**.